F*CK HIM!

Nice Girls Always Finish Last

What you will learn in this book:

The author of this book does not dispense medical advice or prescribe the use of any technique as a form of treatment for physical, emotional or medical problems without the advice of a qualified physician, either directly or indirectly. The intent of the author is only to offer information of a general nature to help you in your quest for emotional and spiritual well-being. In the event you use any of the information in this book, the author and the publisher assume no responsibility for your actions.

Why should you FUCK him?

Let me start off by explaining I am in no way talking about the sexual act. Fuck him in this case is not physical, it's mental.

So many women get in trouble in their love lives, and 99.9 percent of that trouble could have been avoided if they'd said, "Well, fuck him!" a bit more often. Too many women are way too nice and compliant to their men, especially when these men don't deserve that kind of treatment.

And yet, every woman I've ever met tries to not be needy or wear her heart on her sleeve. She simply wants to protect her feelings. Nevertheless, most women I've coached have had men seem very interested only to disappear suddenly. These women are left standing in the dark. Once the guy vanishes, they often find out it's easier to get the President of the United States on the phone than the man who seemingly really liked them...just not enough to stick around.

This should stop.

I, as a dating coach and author of books for women who want to get men, cannot take it anymore. You deserve better. This is not your fault. It's his! He needs to learn to be much more transparent and upfront. That said, we both know most men won't change. We can lead a horse to water, but we can't make it drink. Or can we? What if there was a way to change a guy's behavior? What if you could get into his head and take over the driver's wheel? What if you could make him do more of the things that you appreciate and need and less of the bad behaviors you dislike? At first, this might seem impossible. Nevertheless,

I'm sure you've already met women who are good at manipulating their men.

Enter the high-value woman. You know her. You've seen her. She's the woman who always has great men drooling over her. It's the woman you see getting all the attention. You often wonder, "How does she do it? What do they see in her? What does she know that I don't?"

You might have even complained to your girlfriends that men just don't seem to notice what a catch you are. Your girlfriends may have even said, "He doesn't know what he's missing." What if you could *make* him *see* it?

When you look at these high-value women who get their way with men, it might have surprised you that their looks don't seem to matter. The high-value woman can be great looking, average looking, or even bad looking. It doesn't matter. She knows her way around men. She knows how to *mentally* fuck them.

Let me get straight to the point. A great guy can find hundreds of women who will give him what he needs on a physical level. The physical aspect of relationships, although important, is not really special to most men. When a man gets it (sex), his hunger is gone. I'm sure you've seen this plenty of times. That said, men cannot easily find a woman who can fuck them mentally. These women are much more rare. When a guy finds one of these exceptions, he latches on like a clueless fly that chose your windshield wiper as a landing spot prior to you getting on the freeway. It will try to hold on like its life depends on it...because it does. A great guy will not let go of a woman he deems as high value.

You'll see behavior you've never seen from him. He'll start to put in an effort that makes you feel like you're a queen because to him, you are. At first, it will be strange. If you've never truly been in control of a man, it might feel like riding a horse for the first time. But soon, it will make you feel all tingly inside.

I'm not kidding.

There's nothing more powerful than being in a relationship with a guy and having him do exactly what you want while he thinks it was his idea. (This is important, as you'll see. He needs to think *he* is the one in the driver's seat, even though you actually are.)

This book is not about becoming someone you're not or turning your boyfriend into a spineless manslave. It's about your empowerment, about taking back what's yours. No man should ever be able to play games with you, to take you for granted, to treat you even a tiny bit less than you deserve. By the time you've finished this book, this will all be part of your past.

I'm still not kidding.

Some of these high-value women were born with this gift. Most, however, have had to learn it. Most of my clients found me because they had reached their breaking point. They'd had enough. These women noticed that all the relationships they were in, or tried to get in, ended on the same dead-end street. So *they* had to be doing something wrong. *They* had to change something.

You're about to get all of the insights you'll need to really understand men. You'll read all of the tricks to getting men to treat you the way they should and the way you deserve.

The high-value woman knows how to control men. Not in a bad way. Needless to say, they don't achieve this by becoming a nagging dictator in the relationship. Far from it. Nagging is not even in their dictionary. They never nag, yell, or pout. They don't need to. They know a whole range of psychological facts about men that help steer the men they date. You'll also see that they don't become bad women. They treat men with respect at all times just as they expect respect in return. And that's exactly what they get—a man who doesn't even think about playing games, who values their time, and most importantly, their heart.

Furthermore, these women are best at repelling bad men—men who won't bring anything to the table in the relationship. They're also great at spotting dishonest men who try to play games or hide their real motives.

Are you curious to find out how they do it? Then read on!

How come I know this "high-value woman" so well?

I've met and seen her countless times. I've been coaching people all over the world since 2005. I've written a couple of best-selling books, have coaching courses and programs and for a select group of people do some personal coaching. The only way to give so many people massive value is to know why people do what they do. To get to that point, I've made it my habit, starting in the early 2000s, to interview hundreds of people every year. I ask them for their secrets, I ask them why they believe they are in a happy relationship and why they stepped out of previous ones. As I continued to do this, I started to see a line of recurring strategies used by people who were very successful in finding and keeping a great relationship. I noticed high-value women were all using the same mindset. There were several similar behaviors and strategies. After interviewing close to a thousand of them over the years, I started to explain these strategies to the women I personally coach.

The results were massive.

That's why I decided to write this book. Even though I've already authored several others, I wanted to write a book that solely focuses on how the high-value woman would behave in a set of situations. I also write this book because so many other guides and self-help books on the market are riddled with mistruths; women who claim to know how men think have written these books. These authors have no idea, as proven by the examples used within their pages.

I get it. They want to sugarcoat everything and include insights about men; they want to make sure women *enjoy* reading the book. That makes sense. However, when the information is dead wrong, it's not helping anyone.

Nevertheless, if you've read any of my books, then you'll know I use a different approach: I tell it like it is. I respect women so much that I'm sick and tired of the games some men play. But what bothers me even more are the women who lose out on a great relationship because they don't get the reactions of the guy they're with and lose him as a consequence.

You can expect me to step on your toes here and there throughout this book. Some of what I'll say will be blunt, even hard to take. Please realize that I do this because I have the utmost respect for women, for you. I love and appreciate women more than you will ever know. That's exactly the reason why I chose to be blunt in writing this book. I want you to see men for what they really are, but I also want you to see some of the misguided behaviors that can get a woman in trouble in her love life. Most men have not been honest with you, often in an effort to not hurt your feelings. Sometimes they were just playing games and didn't care at all. That's why I want to tell you the cold, hard truth. That's why I write books. I want to lift the veil so you can see clearly from now on.

Can you handle the truth?

Let's go!
Brian

Why men find the "good girl" or the "nice girl" repelling

You might have noticed that nice girls always finish last, and men seem to prefer bad women. Why would that be?

Imagine a guy who wears white socks during sex. He has a unibrow and looks like he accidently swallowed a bowling ball. As if that's not enough, it's a guy who thinks deodorant is optional. Did I mention he still lives with his mother? It's quite all right. He has a midnight curfew since he's already over thirty-five and all... I think you get where I'm going with this.

Might it be possible this guy will give you the creeps?

Well, that's exactly how men feel when they're with an overly nice, good girl. Even when she's super attractive! Granted, it will take a couple of weeks before he'll get the feeling, but believe me, it will come.

Well, to this I say, "fuck him!" Men are stupid. I can vouch for this, since I'm one myself. We're wired in a weird way, totally illogical when it comes to romance, love, and relationships. You might wonder, "So what are you saying? Can I never be *good* to a guy? Will I be doomed to singledom forever because I am a *good* girl?"

It depends what you mean by *good*. Let me give you the profile of the good/nice girl that men start to dislike.

1. She's looking for the one. I know, we all are. Men as well! But that's not all. Not only is she looking for the one, she also quickly believes she has found him. And this last part is the big mistake.

These nice girls have been with a man for a couple of weeks and then start to make a big deal out of the relationship. They quickly ask where *this* is going. They also accept not-so-great behavior (even though they might complain about it) and keep hoping he will change. She hopes that one day he'll see how great she is and treat her accordingly. These nice girls cannot help it.

One of the consequences of this characteristic is this woman quickly goes all-in and treats him like a king even though he doesn't treat *her* like a queen. Moreover, some nice girls put him *so* high on a pedestal that they think better of him than even he thinks of himself.

2. She tries to impress him when it should be the other way around. The nice girl often has a deeply engrained belief that she is not enough. So she must compensate by being nice or overly supportive and kind. There's no faster way to devalue yourself than by trying to impress him. This action, by definition, proves to him that you believe you're beneath him. A man should always look up to his woman; he should never look down on her.

Suppose I met you in a bar and tried to impress you by jiggling the keys to my Porsche and that I told you I'm an investment banker who makes a gazillion dollars a year. Chances are, your radar is going to sound loud and clear. You may think, "What's the catch?" or "Why does he feel he's not enough? Maybe he *is* not enough!" Trying to impress you in this way, I've immediately devalued myself.

When a woman tries to impress a man she's been with for less than a couple of months, she immediately devalues herself. It really should be the other way around! He should be trying to impress you! I'll show you how to get there later on in this book.

Remember, your actions define how valuable he thinks you are. If you continuously try to give him everything he (might) want, there's nothing left to chase. He will have to go looking for that chase somewhere else.

Do not give a man what he wants. As counter intuitive as this may sound, the more you try to please him by giving him what he wants (even what he says he wants), the more you're devaluing yourself. Granted, if he's going all in and treating you really well, you should put in an effort too. I'll discuss that in detail later.

3. She seeks his approval and tries to please him. This would be the total opposite of the "fuck him" attitude. Seeking his approval puts a ticking time bomb on his feelings and attraction toward a woman. By seeking his approval, a nice girl will position herself beneath him. That's wrong. The king and queen are supposed to be equal.

If he's not a gentleman, he'll run as fast as he can. If he *is* a gentleman, he'll try to hold on a little longer but will eventually leave as well.

Most men won't communicate any of this to you. Most men disappear or use excuses like "I'm not ready for a *serious* relationship" (but then they get married a couple of months later to a new woman they've just met).

They believe they're helping the woman by not being transparent in an effort to avoid hurting her feelings. First of all, of course they've just hurt her feelings. What are these men thinking? Second, they're not doing her any favors because chances are this poor good girl is going to continue making the same mistakes with every guy she meets since every guy says she's not the problem. And none of these men have the balls to tell her what *really* happened. Well, to this I say, fuck him.

4. She lets him call the shots. Men truly are interested in the nice girl, at first. Jamie, one of my clients, was a nice girl. At 57 and after a nasty divorce 23 years earlier, she finally met another great man who swept her away. He was handsome, wealthy, successful, and above all, very respectful and kind. She had never ever met a guy like him. He called her daily, took her out on great dates, pulled out her chair, held the door open for her...

After three months of dating, he took her to a nice restaurant. During dinner he kneeled and took out a nice little black box from his jacket. He popped it open and to Jamie's delight, a very shiny and seemingly expensive diamond was lighting up her eyes.

"Jamie, I've never ever met a woman like you before. I feel like I'm 17 again, and I want to feel like this forever. Will you marry me?" he asked. Jamie, totally dazzled, felt as if she was in one of those princess fairy tales and quickly nodded her head.

Four weeks later, as the first wedding preparations had started, Jamie got a call from her fiancé: "Jamie, look, we've got to talk. Can we meet up?" Jamie was about to be dazzled again...

Her fiancé explained that everything was going too fast, and he wanted to call off the wedding. He was not ready for a new relationship and wanted to stop seeing her.

Can you see what went wrong here?

It's not that obvious. Everything seemed too great! Jamie never nagged, never pushed. Jamie never did anything. She went along for the ride. And *that's* exactly the problem. She let him call all of the shots. He went all-in way too fast, and Jamie let him. He then got spooked and ran away like a little boy who just saw a spider on his pillow.

A man needs to think he's calling the shots, but truthfully, you should be the one steering the relationship. The nice girl hands over her power and her heart to the man she loves way too quickly. She does this to the bad men, but as you saw here, also to the good men.

There is a different approach, however. Let's dig into this in the next chapter.

The high-value woman never plays games

Men are always looking for challenges. All great men who have ever lived were chasing after multiple achievements, goals, and milestones throughout their lives. Men can chase money, fame, women, a title, all of the above, and more. Chasing they will.

The high-value woman knows this all too well. She considers herself to be a prize—one he needs to chase after. She will not always be available; she will not always answer his calls; she will most often not give him what he wants. Yet, she doesn't play any games either.

Can you see why?

If she were to play games, a great and smart man would see right through them. Games are an effort to make a man like you more. Games are a way to get his approval.

A woman who plays games is perceived as weak by great guys who, again, see right through them. The nanosecond men know a woman is doing something under the radar in an effort to be liked, they lose all the value they had been building. What do you feel when you realize a guy is on his knees, trying to kiss your feet to get you to like him more? It's a feeling nobody likes.

When the high-value woman doesn't have time for him, it's not a game. She truly doesn't have time for him because she has other important stuff to attend to... even if it's just reorganizing her sock drawer. When she doesn't answer his call right away, it's not because she wants to make him wait. It's because she really does have something more important to do first.

This behavior fucks with him. Big time. He's left wondering, "Wow, this is the first woman I've called who didn't call me back right away" or "Wow, this is the first woman I've asked out on a second date, after a great first date might I say, who didn't jump on the opportunity. She even asked to postpone it a couple of days because she's busy." This is the challenge all men are looking for. All men. Even those who claim they don't like it. If there weren't a chance of losing, men would not love winning so much!

This doesn't just apply in the beginning of the relationship, mind you. All along the life the two of you will spend together. That's why it's so important to not play games. You can't keep them up anyway. All of this has to be real. He has to fall for the *real* you. I'll teach you how later on.

You've heard it a gazillion times: "Just be yourself!" Question is, who is that exactly? What does this mean? Is a needy woman who nags still herself? No, she's not. He's bringing out the worst in her, and she lets it happen! The high-value woman won't let him transform her into a nagger. She holds the cards over herself at all times.

Mental Fucking

When it comes to fucking a man, there are two rules.

Rule number one: never share your body with him too soon. There are multiple reasons for this. The crucial one is that you'll fall in love way too hard, way too soon. Dr. Breuning, Professor Emerita at California State University, explained this very well in *Psychology Today*.[1] When a man touches a woman (yes, one intimate touch is enough) and definitely after sex, she gets the love hormone called oxytocin rushing through her body. This is a very tricky and deceptive little hormone. It's nature's way of creating a bond between you and that man. Nature doesn't know contraceptives exist, so after sex, a woman might become pregnant. That's why it's imperative the guy sticks around to protect and provide for the mother and child. So she gets oxytocin. The effects of oxytocin, however, are where the traps lie.

Dr. Breuning confirms oxytocin will make you evaluate others more positively (than they might be). On top of that, oxytocin tells a woman "this is the one." And that's a trap. The oxytocin hasn't lived with that guy for five years yet; it didn't spend time with him during the good *and* the bad periods of his life, and it didn't check whether he respects her or takes her for granted, whether he cleans up after himself, etc. It did none of that homework! So if the woman falls for what the oxytocin makes her feel, she's stuck in the trap. And more importantly, her clingy behavior will soon become too intimidating to the guy, causing him to run.

----

[1] https://www.psychologytoday.com/blog/love-and-gratitude/201310/oxytocin-the-love-and-trust-hormone-can-be-deceptive

And it's not even her fault! The clingy behavior is a pure consequence of that darn oxytocin.

Long story short, don't sleep with him too soon or learn how to look past the blinders the oxytocin will give. The first part is way easier than the second, so that's your safest bet.

Another major reason why you shouldn't share your bed with him too soon is you've just given him a precious asset. You are without a doubt so much more than your body! I know you probably are a great friend and trustworthy person with a riveting personality and so much more to offer. But *he* doesn't know that yet.

When a man walks up to you or goes out on a date, it's not because of your personality! He thinks you're physically attractive. I'm here to tell you the truth. Men don't care about your personality at first. Every single man who asks for your digits is purely interested in your body. Every man who stays with you after ten dates or so does so for your personality. It's only after a couple months of dating that he starts to realize what a great person you are. Men are superficial at first. So don't give him what he wants too soon. Work on that emotional connection first.

So the first rule of fucking a man is don't share your body too soon.

Rule number two: mentally fuck him as soon as you can! Not only will this force him to look past your body, it will create the mental challenge men so desperately need. Let me emphasize this. You can wait at least ten dates to have him see your personality, or you can speed up the process and force him to see the real you from the get go.

You'll need to do this soon! From the first second you meet him. It's imperative to be sassy and savvy and high value. When he's out on a first date with you or has just walked up to you, he likes you physically. That first physical impression has been formed the moment he saw you. The more important first impression of your personality, however, is still being formed while you're talking to him. And the sooner you get this right, the harder he will fall for you.

If you want him to treat you like a queen, act like a queen right out of the gate. No exceptions. I'll get into the nitty gritty later in this book, but I want to emphasize that I use the word queen deliberately. No man wants a princess. A princess still doesn't know what she wants, is emotionally unstable, and makes men uncomfortable. She acts young and flakey. The queen, however, knows what she wants, understands exactly how she wants to be treated, and will not accept any bad behavior. Period. The men who mistakenly believe they can disrespect her get to spend the rest of their lives in the cold, dark, and moldy dungeon.

Let's dive into the importance of this rule. If you fuck him mentally, he will look past your body. This is the very reason you'll see average-looking women with super great guys. This strategy is one of their secrets. Some of the men they're with might not have had any physical attraction for them at first, but these sassy women cultivated it through that strong mental challenge they represent.

So how does one mentally fuck him? You fuck him mentally when you leave him startled because of your behavior. Bad behavior (e.g., nagging and complaining) doesn't startle men who've had a relationship or two. They expect it! They know it will come and simply use it as a cue to put their hooks out and find a new fish in the sea.

That's when the nice girls hears, "Yeah, I'm not sure I'm ready for something serious, and I don't want to hurt your feelings later on." Just as most women have triggers to finding a guy repulsive, men are conditioned as well. They have been in bad relationships before and want to avoid living through those same experiences like the plague.

High-value women do it differently. They startle him with some or all of the following behaviors:

- Instead of falling head over heels for him, she decides what she feels (oxytocin) are just feelings. Feelings come and go. She doesn't get infatuated. Any man she meets is on probation first, regardless of what her feelings tell her. She's not hesitant or guarding herself; she simply doesn't crown him the king before he has earned it.

- She wants a relationship but not just any relationship. She's happy to stay single for as long as necessary. If she stays single for the rest of her life, then she'll still have fun and make the most of it. She realizes her neediness simply comes from her natural instincts that have been programmed to "get a man and make babies" (even though she might be 40 or 60 and babies are the last thing on her rational mind). She knows this is just her primitive programming, and she surpasses that. She would love to be in a great relationship but not so much that she would devalue herself. She never ever *needs* a man or a relationship.

- Instead of hooking on to any man she meets and following all of those primitive instincts, she consciously wonders, "Is this the best guy to give my time to?" Here too she'll have to surpass her primitive emotions, partially fueled by hormones like oxytocin. She uses her emotional intelligence, looks at the long term, and asks herself, "If this guy never changed, would I really want to be with him ten or twenty years from now?" *She* is the one who's still weighing all of his pros and cons. He feels it and starts to put in the hard, necessary work to gain *her* approval.

- She knows she might not be the prettiest woman he could get. She was never the prom queen; she doesn't look like a model, and when she goes out, most men hover around some of her other girlfriends. She doesn't care. She *really* doesn't. These are not the types of men she wants anyway. Plus, she knows she doesn't need her looks to get a great guy. Looks will fade at some point. She wants her man to be addicted to her personality. As a result, when she's dating she doesn't ask questions like: "Do you think I'm pretty?" or "What was your ex like?" If a guy was with her just for her looks, she would walk away anyway. She wants more from a relationship than this superficial stuff. She knows she's a queen, not a princess.

- When the first date was great, she doesn't text him afterward to let him know it was fun. She's busy with her life, and she'll see when and if he contacts her again. If he doesn't, she won't reach out to him! She only wants men who are sufficiently interested. She has 24 hours in a day, just like anyone else, of which she takes about 8 hours to sleep, 10 hours or so to work on her career, 1 hour to drive to and from work (if she's lucky), 1 hour to walk or work out...that only leaves so much time. She knows she needs to spend it wisely. She looks at the ROI of her time. She doesn't want to spend it on some guy who's not putting in the hard work she deserves. If he's more than ten minutes late for their date without calling her to exactly tell her why (and there better be a good reason!), she's gone. If he wants to make it up to her, he can, but it better be good (a home cooked meal, for instance).

I think you get the point. She places high value on her life, her heart, and her time. She wants the return on her time investment to be high, and she'll let him know that, in a kind way, from the get-go.

Being kind is crucial here. She never behaves like a bitch. She's kind but firm and strict. She brings her best self to the table and expects the same from her guy. When he fails to deliver, she'll let him know right away. For example, she may say, "I had fun the first couple of dates, and I really like you, but I can't be with a guy who... (fill in some behavior you don't like)." She says this instead of complaining, "Why don't you ever..." That's the take-it-or-leave-it mentality she holds dearly.

The first couple of weeks of your interaction with a man set the stage. Whatever is set is difficult to change or remove later on. Men know this!

Did you ever really study how a three-year-old kid behaves around his mother? He tests her diligently and perpetually! He'll continuously test her limits to see what he can get away with. Grown-up men are no different. From the get-go they'll tease, play, and see what they can get away with.

Here's a little secret. The ideal woman to most men allows him to be the dictator in the relationship; she obeys his every command. When he wants sex, she gives it in any way he likes. When he's hungry, she prepares him a five-course meal. When he's watching TV and wants a beer, she'll get him a cold one and prepares a little snack too, just in case he's hungry. She totally ignores the fact that he's getting a huge beer belly because of all those beers, and she continues to adore him physically. She continuously repeats that he's the answer to her prayers. She even wonders out loud whether he *is* God, given his perfect abilities to do...well, just about anything. That's what most men think they want.

Until they get it. Then they run.

Let's look at a different scenario that will provide great insight into how the mind of a man works. Suppose that in option one, a guy can get a job where he has a fixed salary of 10,000 dollars a month, every single month, year in and year out. His job performance is of no importance. Whether he shows up on time, or at all, doesn't matter. He gets his salary every single month, paid on time.

Let's look at option two. In option two, our guy gets a salary of 10,000 dollars a month, but he has to work for it! He has to show up on time, put in a good performance, follow seminars to get better, read books, and improve. If he does all of this diligently, his salary will be paid every month.

Option one would sound like a dream to most guys! And probably to you too. What a life! But as a woman, you're smart enough to look past this. What most guys don't see—until they experience it—is that option one is boring. Only a few months into this scenario, he'll start to take his salary for granted. He'll be bored, even though this money allows him to buy most of the stuff he's dreamt about for a long time. It has no value since there was no challenge. He doesn't have to work for it.

The second option, on the other hand, keeps him motivated and on his A-game. He values the money so much more because he's had to work hard for it, month after month. I know there are exceptions, there are a lot of lazy couch-potato men out there too, but I'm guessing that's not the type of guy you're interested in anyway.

This is why the high-value woman is so attractive, especially to ambitious men who long for success. Those are the men programmed to work for what they want. And when they don't have to, whatever they were chasing gets devalued to below zero.

What remains important is that the high-value woman doesn't play games. So this is not a ploy to get him to bend over and behave the way she wants. It is simply the only way that's acceptable to her! Everything she says and does will prove her value, will prove that she *will* walk away when he takes her for granted (he won't), when he doesn't treat her with respect (he might try, but then she's gone).

And she shows this from the very first second they meet. She'll be sassy in her responses when he teases her. She'll be assertive and strict when he tries to push or play her. She'll stop giving him attention altogether when he shows undesirable behavior.

And she does it from the start. I cannot emphasize this enough. So many women I've coached during the last ten years got this wrong. When he did something wrong, these women thought, "Well, I can't start nagging now. I'll just keep it to myself. He'll change later, and if he doesn't, I'll try to change him (by nagging)." Needless to say, this is a very bad strategy. He won't understand where this is all coming from ("This wasn't a problem when we first started dating. Why is it one now?"), and by that time, he has devalued her so much that he simply doesn't care anymore. The nagging will go on for some time, and he still won't change (or he will rebound after a temporary change in an effort to evade the nagging). Then he'll be gone. This can be avoided by showing what's important to you from the get-go, without nagging. I'll give you the tactical details in a later chapter.

A relationship will always be based upon habits. If you create a habit where he doesn't have to put in an effort at first, why would he change later? If sex is easy to get, why would he diligently work for it later? If he doesn't need to treat you well, take you out, buy you flowers, put his best foot forward to get your attention and affection, why would he all of a sudden start doing this later?

Create the right habits as soon as you can.

Why do women fall for bad boys?

That's a question I've pondered about day in and day out before starting my career as a dating coach. Why do women fall for bad boys? And more importantly, why do some women stay with a bad boy when it's obvious she's never ever going to get what she wants or deserves from *that* guy?

Mind you, this is not just a trap for women with a below average IQ. I've seen very smart women stay with men who disrespected them daily. It took them weeks, sometimes months, before they could walk away.

There are a ton of superficial reasons for this, but they all boil down to one thing; even though humans are intelligent creatures, we're still governed by our primal instincts— much more than we'd like to admit.

Dr. Breuning concluded her research by stating some women's primal instincts are *so* strong that their entire body believes these bad men will be able to protect them better than the nice guys. This primal instinct causes a woman to believe she needs protection. That was true until one hundred years ago, when every woman who wanted to make babies and live a long and healthy life *needed* a man to take care of her and protect her.

And even today, this is still partially true. According to the World Health Organisation, as many as 35 percent of women worldwide have experienced sexual violence in their lifetime. And these are just the women who report it. This still blows my mind. Needless to say, there's a very good reason why your primal instinct wants you to be protected by a man who loves you and would give his life to protect yours when needed.

If you have a tendency to fall for bad guys, now you know why. Even though they treat you badly, your body thinks they will protect you better than those nice but weaker guys. Bad boys seem to ooze with self-confidence, and that's exactly what fires your primal instincts. That said, the well-sculpted guys are often exactly the ones who have the least self-esteem. Narcissists are part of this group, too. They are *very* bad for you but have become masters at hiding their true selves in the early stages of the relationship. They know exactly how to trigger a woman's primal instincts to get her stuck in their traps.

You won't be able to change your primal instincts, but you *can* explain to yourself why it's happening and that you shouldn't listen to it.

Let's dive into some of the ways he might trigger your primal instincts in the next chapter.

Is he playing games with me?
Why and how men test their women

There are different types of men. As I described in my book *Red Flags, Signs He's Playing Games With You*, a lot of men who play games are really bad for you. I've described how to spot them in that book. Here, however, I want to focus on the good guys.

What if you're in a relationship with a guy and he pulls back, or he says he'll call and then doesn't, or he is late for a date? Is he playing games? A good guy, even a gentleman, might deliberately pull any of those off indeed. And when he does, it's a test!

He's testing you to see what personality you really have. This is partially the three-year-old kid in him, who just wants to see what he can get away with (it'd better not be too much), but more importantly, he's trying to see how you will respond.

Just like you probably have had, the men you'll meet will have had their fair share of bad dates and relationships, possibly even a bad marriage...or two. He may have scars and small to major emotional trauma. This would put up anyone's guard. That's why some men, not all, will decide to test you. To see how you will behave, how you will react.

Some of the tests he can deploy are:

- 1. Telling you he'll call, but then he doesn't
- 2. Being more aloof and thus creating some distance
- 3. "Honestly" telling you that he's not ready for a relationship

alling asleep right after sex. No, I'm kidding, at's real and not a test. All men have had this ᴇaction, even to the best sex ever...especially to the ᴅest sex ever.

. he puts you through any of these tests early on (within the first couple of months of dating), he'll closely monitor your reactions. Let's go over the wrong way and the right way for those first three tests mentioned above.

1. When he says he'll call and then doesn't, some women who finally do get a hold of him will snap at him. When you read between the lines, you'll notice this woman is clearly communicating he's very important to her, she has been worrying about when she'd finally get through to him, and now, she's mad. There's no challenge for him as a result. He has her. This will reassure *and* scare him at the same time. And that last part is important. Some men test a woman just to see where they stand. But even when they get the confirmation, they'll get scared. Did I already mention that men are totally illogical when it comes to emotions and romance?

   The right way to respond is to not care. The high-value woman would not care for real. She has several passion projects, even small things like gardening, walking, reorganizing the plants in her fishbowl. She has so many activities that she doesn't even sense it when he takes a step back. Even if she does, she thinks, "Well, fine. If he doesn't like me enough then I'll find me a guy who does. I deserve nothing less!"

   So upon taking his call or seeing him after a period of total silence, she'll act like nothing has happened. To her, nothing has. He, on the other hand, will not find the reassurance he might have been looking for, which will make him chase her harder. But his alarm bells won't go off either. He won't see her as the needy woman every man runs away from. This will make him feel closer to her.

If you've never tested this, please do. Men react like Pavlov's dog. I know I do. Our emotional wiring isn't all that complicated. That's exactly the problem for some women; they try to make it complicated when men are in fact pretty easy to steer once you know how.

2. When he creates distance by disappearing from the radar, some women will chase after him. That's never a good idea. It will not only turn him off, but more importantly, it lowers their self-respect tremendously. The high-value woman reacts by putting more of her attention into other passions, or even other men she then starts dating, even if this guy still lingers around in her head. (She's not a robot after all; she does have feelings.)

   She knows she's good enough. If *he* can't see it, someone else will. She only wants a guy who wants her for who she is. If she has to start chasing him, work out more, lose weight, get a nose job, dye her hair, get rid of her cat or whatever to get him, he's not the king she wants. And she doesn't let him know by nagging, she does so by not paying attention to him. The men who are not sufficiently interested will disappear, and that's great (less time wasted). But the good guys will surprise you. They will start to chase, work out, lose weight, and maybe even *get* a cat just to get into your good graces again.

   I want to repeat again that this is *not* some game to her. She has forced herself to believe that she is enough. And if a certain guy doesn't see it? NEXT! As I said, most women were not born with this gift. They've had to reprogram their own beliefs. They kept repeating it until it became a habit to react that way.

As I always say, you are the most important person you will ever meet! You've been there for you since day one, and you'll be there for you during your final moments. It's OK to treat yourself as such, as the important person you are to yourself. I realize this may sound silly or obvious. But if you look into it, you'll see there surely are some areas in your life where you're not fully embracing this concept.

When a woman doesn't act like she finds herself important, he won't find her important either.

3. Another test he might deploy is telling you he's not ready for a relationship. That's an interesting one! I've coached women who had a man say this. Their response? They became needy! He then repeated he really wasn't ready and didn't want to lead them on...as he was breaking up with them. Less than a year later, he married his dream girl. I've seen this happen to so many women!

    It is *no* coincidence. When a man uses that sentence, he's trying to create some space. What he's really saying is that he likes her, but he wants to take things slow so he can get comfortable with all of these feelings and emotions that men simply cannot handle well. Mind you, I'm still talking about the good guys here; there are, of course, men who use this phrase to lead women on.

So how can you know the difference? By responding exactly in the way the high-value woman would. She says, "Sure, take all the time you need. I'm not sure about you either."

The man then thinks, "Say what? You're not sure? Why not?" This will intrigue him and make him want her more. I repeat, men are not all that complicated.

Here's the rule. While staying kind and respectful, the more you ignore him or make it not important where "this" goes, the more he will want you! The more he will want "this" to go somewhere. You can think this is silly, childish, and absolutely ridiculous (it is). But this is reality. When does a three-year-old boy seek the attention of his mommy? When she's paying attention to something or someone else, when she's ignoring him.

Adult men are no different.

If he has feelings for you, then the less important you think he is, the more important he will believe you to be. The high-value woman draws in men like moths to a flame because she will never find him or the relationship *as* important as he does. When you study her and the way she acts in relationships, you'll see that he's always one step ahead when it comes to how important the relationship is.

Let's look at these scenarios. On a scale from one to ten, here's how important the relationship is to:

Man: 6, Woman: 10 > The man will get suffocated and will run.

Woman: 6, Man: 10 > It will take longer, but the woman will start to see her guy as her friend/brother. Although she might not run, she'll soon discover she's attracted to other men.

Am I right? When you look at your past relationships or those of people you know, you'll see this dynamic to be true. She/he who *needs* the relationship the most doesn't have the lead. However, he/she who *needs* the relationship the least will perpetually keep attracting the other party.

I deliberately use the word need instead of want. It's OK to want a relationship; most of us do. But the person who needs a relationship will always have the weaker position simply because he/she has the most to lose.

It's easy to act needy, to overcompensate, to seek approval, to accept bad behavior, and to make any of the other mistakes if you really *need* the relationship. That's what the high-value woman does so well. She wants the man she's with. He *needs* the woman he's with. She gets him hooked because of her behavior. And you can take this literally. She creates some form of an addiction where he just couldn't imagine his life without her.

To get there, she does many little things that I will describe throughout this book, but it always comes down to these three traits:

1. She's a queen. She believes she is high value, regardless of what anyone else thinks. She has a lot of self-respect.

2. He's not the epicenter of her life. She loves him dearly, but her life never revolves around him. He can come along for the ride, or they can both go for a ride and decide what destination to head to, but she's never in the passenger seat.

3. She never ever pursues him. If he seems to lose interest, she withdraws. She has better things to do. She loves being in a relationship, but she doesn't need it to be happy and fulfilled.

Your most powerful weapon

You have one very powerful weapon toward men. Your looks.

That's what you expected me to say, right?

It's wrong. Your looks don't matter nearly as much as you think. There are plenty of gorgeous women with a love life from hell. While there are several normal-looking women married to great guys who adore them.

Having great looks only gets your foot in the door. Men use your looks to decide whether they will walk up to you or not. But they do not want to marry your looks, move in with your looks, make babies with your looks. No, no. They want *you*, the whole package.

Truth be told, I've seen girlfriends of mine become gorgeous when I got to know them better. Truly. If I had to be blunt and score them on their looks, I would have given them a 6 or a 7 on a scale from 1 to 10. When I was dating them and got to know their great personalities, however, they quickly rose to a 10 or above.

I want to emphasize that love makes men blind as well! These women actually became gorgeous in my eyes. If I were to be at a networking party full of models and actresses, I would still have thought my girlfriend to be the most gorgeous and attractive one. That's because she was, to me.

Something magical happens when you show a man the real you. Not the part of you that might want to seek approval, be needy, or nag. That's never the real you; that's just an insecure part of yourself. All of this is tricky. If this were easy, no woman would have a problem holding onto that great guy she likes.

One of the major problems is most women have been led to believe that all men want is sex. You've probably read eye-catching claims like, "Men think about sex every six seconds" or "Get a sexy stomach in no time flat" and "Inject nasty stuff into your lips so you'll start looking like a sex doll!" These are taught to women from an early age by the magazines that scream what women should be doing to be lovable.

Some women sadly never understand that all these magazines want to do is sell more magazines. The editors don't care about your love life or about you.

Here's the cold, hard truth:
-   Men have a huge drive to make babies. Not to be a daddy, change diapers, play happy family. They merely want to have sex and make babies. It's in their instincts. They want to spread their genes and reproduce. They have been programmed to. For this, men do not, I repeat, *do not* think about sex all the time! Yet, a lot of what they do is to get sex indeed!

Allow me to explain as we dive deeper inside the male mind. What I'm about to share has been scientifically researched by Geoffrey Miller, author of *The Mating Mind* and *Spent.* He found out that almost everything men do is to get sex.

When men chase money or success, they do this to be able to get a great woman. When men buy a Porsche, they want to be important and attract women. Sure, we all know how you'd fall right away for a guy who steps out of a

Porsche...right? Men are so primitive and silly sometimes. Almost everything they buy is to attract the right women. If we look at it like this, men indirectly think about sex *every* single second of their day.

And yet, sex is not *that* important to him. When a man hasn't had sex for a while, hormones start to build in his body; his urge will get bigger and bigger. Until he gets sex or pleases himself by watching porn or by simply using his imagination.

If having sex with an actual woman were the only way to release that urge, to take the steam out of the kettle, bad things would start to happen in the world. Luckily, men have other ways to clean the pipes. And that's what sex is.

When he has sex with *you*, however, it's supposed to be a lot more than just helping him get rid of his urge. It should be, and it can be. But it's up to you to decide! If you give him sex too soon, it will be just about sex. You won't be anything more than all of the other women he's only had sex with.

If, however, you make him wait for it, you can build up your value a lot. It's the best way to quickly put you into the category with high-value women. I already explained that men will test you and try to define your personality by looking at your behavior. Holding out on sex is very strong behavior. And it's good for you, too! It's the best way to weed out some of the game players just looking for one-night stands or friends with benefits. You'll never have those guys just for yourself, so it's best to filter them out quickly.

What's interesting though is that men will decide what category they put you in (one-night stand versus relationship material) long before they've had sex with you. So besides not having sex too soon (definitely not the first 3-4 dates), try to steer clear of the following:

- Do not use your body to lure him. Don't hide it, but don't use it either. Make him wonder. There's a reason why strippers don't walk up to the stage already naked. They are well dressed and then take their clothes off one piece at a time, very slowly. This builds the anticipation. The visual aspect is important too. Men are much more visual than women when it comes to arousal. You know this. But this doesn't mean a woman should show everything. His imagination is visual, too. Give him visual hints, without showing the goods. A man will find it a lot sexier if you wear a shirt or sweater that somewhat shows the shape of your breasts than walking around bare-breasted. Even showing cleavage too soon is not a good idea. Show him shapes, not the actual body part.

- Here's another trick you can use. I'll never forget when I was about 14 years old, full on in my puberty and hornier than a bull. I had a young and pretty math teacher. She was always well dressed and took care of her appearance. One day she had been sitting at her desk as we completed an assignment. She was wearing a classy skirt and shirt, with her hair in a ponytail. Then she dropped a pen and bent over to pick it up. For a split second I could look up her shirt that was loosely hanging down. I saw her bra. This drove me nuts. My hormones went berserk for the very first time ever. This was also the very first time I had felt one of the powers a woman can have over a guy. She gave me a hint. My mind couldn't stop thinking about the complete picture. Had she given me the complete picture by standing totally naked in front of the blackboard, I would not have been thinking about her in that way for months. To be honest, even thinking about that moment now, more than twenty years later, still does something to me. There are many ways you can give him a hint. However, it should be inconspicuous. If he realizes you're doing it on purpose, it will lose ALL of its power. All of it! It devalues you right away to the one-night-stand category. Trying (too) hard never works well on a man. Please remember they always want what they cannot get (right away) or that for which they have to work hard.

So here are some great examples of hints:

- Hang/put something sexy of you somewhere in your home where he can see it. Make sure it's the usual place for that item to not make it obvious. An example is hanging one of your sexy bras on the back of your bathroom door. Placing some sexy shoes where he will take his shoes off. He will then start to visualize you wearing that item. Always build up the anticipation first.

- When it's time to say goodnight after the first or the second and even the third date, he might invite you over. If he's audacious, he'll invite himself in either directly or with a ruse. Even though your entire body might be screaming to have sex with him then and there, don't. You can say, "I'm not ready for this yet. You'll need to pass a couple more tests first" with a big smile. This is flirty, playful, and will allow him to build up the anticipation and chase you harder. Most importantly, it will give you the time to really gauge his personality before being blinded by the oxytocin rush after having had sex with him.

- Wear something that shows your sexy shapes, without showing too much skin (or any skin at all). Keep him guessing.

Women who are overtly sexual aren't sexy at all. Trying to be sexy never ever *is* sexy. It's perceived as weakness by most men. Sure, they might still be attracted to it, but it will only stand for one night.

Holding off is always a good idea because it will increase the price of the reward. Guess for which woman he will continue to put his best foot in? The woman who gives him great sex every day, or the woman who he can conquer once or twice a week? The harder it is to get something, the more he will appreciate it. It also seriously increases your value since he'll know you don't sleep around.

Speaking of sleeping around, when you sleep with a guy too soon, he'll immediately think you do that with *all* men you meet. Even though he might truly be the exception and you clearly say so, he won't think so. No man wants to be with a woman he believes all men can get. It has no value to him, no matter how good she looks. It will feel good during sex, but he'll start to have second thoughts the very millisecond his orgasm is over.

I'll never forget what happened to a great friend of mine, John. He's an average-looking guy with a balding head. We were at a networking event filled with interesting people. He started to chat with a truly gorgeous woman. He gets her phone number, calls her the next day, and asks her out for Friday that same week. She says yes, they have a great date, and she sleeps with him right away. That Sunday, we go to the gym to work out. He tells me he's not sure he wants to continue seeing her. I ask him why. His exact words were, "I don't know. I don't really *know* her, but I'm already bored of her." I asked, "Was the sex not great? I mean, she looked gorgeous." He immediately responded, "Sure! The sex was awesome. She's really hot, and she was open to anything I wanted. Anything."

I already knew what was going on, why he disliked her, but I dug a little deeper. "And you don't want more of *that*?" I asked. "Sure, if I don't meet anyone better, I might hook up with her again," he admitted. "But you know, now that it was *this* easy to get a girl that good looking. Who knows who I can score? I can reach higher than this!"

Yes...I warned you I was going to give you the cold, hard truth. This is what's going on in the deep, dark caves of the male mind. The more successful a guy is, the more he'll want to go to the next level once he has completed the mission at the current level. In every aspect of his life. That's exactly why it's so crucial that he cannot get a woman too soon, and that he never fully gets her at all.

The harder you make it on him (without using any negativity—no nagging or complaining), the more he'll want you. The high-value woman uses this power sparingly of course; she doesn't want to make his life a living hell where he's continuously wondering where he stands with her either.

Before we dive into the next chapter, I want to point out a major mistake that you should avoid.

The hints I discussed should remain hints, nothing more. There's nothing more frustrating to a guy than getting cozy with a woman, starting to make out, hoping that *it* will happen, seeing her get all steamy and hot herself, having her remove his shirt or her blouse or whatever other sign that makes it clear that the birds are about to start chirping, only to have the woman then say, "Stop. I'm not ready yet" or "Stop. I forgot I have to get up early tomorrow" or anything to the same tune that means the fun is over. Try taking a sweet lollipop away from a three-year-old, and you'll see the exact same reaction.

It will be a very bad reaction, emotionally. If your hints are too strong and you allow him to take off like a rocket only to shoot him down minutes later, it will be *so* frustrating to him that he'll link this negative experience to you. If this happens twice, *he* won't be in the mood again next time. He'll be out looking for someone else. He'll prefer not getting anything than feeling *this* again.

When you make his rocket take off, you should always let it reach the moon before it has to return back to earth. That's why it's better to not have any of the first 3-4 dates ending up at your place or his. It's best that your hint' come from things he can see, not your words or actions since those can be misinterpreted.

If he sees your bra hanging on your bathroom door, he's going to get aroused without thinking that you lead him on. If you let him kiss you passionately, allow him to open your blouse, touch your breasts, and only *then* stop him in his tracks, he'll think you lead him on. You'll lose points.

This is why I always advise my clients to not make any sexual innuendos, to not give any sexual hints. Keep the boat off. And don't let him look in the playbook. Don't say, "I don't have sex before the fourth date." This would again take all of the mystery away and who knows, you might not feel ready during the fourth date. You are in the driver's seat here. You'll be ready when you're ready (just not before the third or fourth date, really), and he'll see it when the moment comes. That could be the moment where he has cooked a great meal for you, given you a couple of nice compliments, and has proven to be a good guy. As you're having a conversation in your or his living room, you turn on some music, get up, and ask him to dance. If he does, even though he's a terrible dancer, you hold him close and gently press your breasts against his chest.

As soon as you see he's heating up and getting aroused, you excuse yourself and go to the bathroom where you freshen up a bit. When you return, you unbutton one button of your shirt (only then, in his presence) you start making out and let it go from there. You then let *him* take the lead (he wants to think he's in the lead), but we both know you were in control at all times. He's only getting you because he deserved it, because you're ready.

If you're in a relationship with him, when you're in the mood, go for it. When you're not, don't do him any favors. Sex needs to be earned, and sex needs to be enjoyed by the both of you at all times. Please don't think he's going to run away if you don't give him enough sex. The men who do were game players; they were not in it for the long haul, and you're better off without them.

Men have plenty of ways to get sex. They can find a one-night stand, they can pay for it, they can go get a massage with a weird ending... Great guys love sex, but they *love* making love even more. That's harder to get. The guy who sticks with you for the long term will be all about making love to you. And that's a totally different thing compared to just sex. Men who want to make love to you will wait. They know it's precious.

When a man wants to have sex with you soon, this can be a test too! Here's another secret about men. Most guys are ready to have sex with you the very second they think you are attractive. A five-minute conversation is all most men will need. Some won't even need a conversation at all. A lot of men will try to have sex with you after the first, second, and third date. They'll invite you in, invite themselves in, make sexual innuendos, and use a myriad of strategies to get into your pants. So that must mean they really want you to have sex with them, right?

Wrong.

This can very well be a test! They want to see how quickly you will bend over...figuratively. They want you to say no. Because if and when you do, you've just proven to them you don't sleep around, that it will be a challenge to share the bed sheets with you, and that it will eventually be an honor when you decide *they* are good enough to get you.

Sex is your most powerful weapon. Use it sparingly and wisely.

The counterintuitive way to get him to do whatever you want

Have you ever been with a guy and wondered, "Ah. I really wish he would"...or "I wish he would no longer..."? This is, of course, a rhetorical question. Of course it has! No man is perfect... except in his own eyes.

If you didn't pick an overly nice guy who will be bowing at your feet by the first date, ready to kiss your perfectly manicured toes, ready for your commands, ready to please you 24/7 like an English butler... getting him to do something or change his behavior isn't straightforward.

This makes me think about Janice, a woman I coached a couple of years ago. Janice had attracted a great guy, a lawyer. She was a successful entrepreneur herself and had a chain of retail stores. Mark, the fake name I'll use for her boyfriend, had a very busy schedule. So the two of them only had a couple of hours every week they could spend together, even though they were already living under the same roof at that time.

Mark loved Janice, but he loved his friends too. Every Friday night he would go out with the boys. Janice was free to join them, of course. But she had quickly learned that such a testosterone-filled night was not what she was looking for after a hard week of to-do lists and stress. Sunday afternoons were kept free by Mark to play golf with friends, clients, or prospects.

Janice wanted to spend more quality time together with Mark, and she had addressed this to him often, borderline nagging about it. This made Mark feel very uncomfortable. At first he had tried to stay home more, because Janice asked for it. Nevertheless, Janice soon learned that Mark wasn't really present mentally. He even became *more* distant. A couple of weeks later, he just went golfing again and told her it was important to him. Complaining and nagging didn't work. What other options did Janice have here?

We'll need to look at the three-year-old kid again. If you tell that kid he can't do something, he'll rebel and only want to do it more. Adult men are, again, no different. By telling him he can't do something, you've created a challenge, and that's exactly what will attract him to do it. If you force him to change his behavior, he'll start to resent you for it. He'll feel less happy and will blame that on you. Every time a man *has* to do something for you, you're building up resentment and seriously hurting the feelings he has for you.

Moreover, you'll notice some women keep adding to the list of to-dos.

- "Let me know when you've arrived safely."
- "Let me know when you're coming home from work."
- "Who was that on the phone?"
- "What were you doing?"
- "Who was with you?"
- "Are you really going to wear *that* shirt?"
- "Don't forget to..."

They act just like his mother. Men love their mothers (if they treated them well while they were growing up), but they won't feel attracted to her. They can't. Plus, they only have room for one mother in their lives. They don't need another one. They need a woman they can be passionately attracted to and in love with. The more rules and to-dos you give him, the more he will feel suffocated. And as I'm sure you know, men have a very low tolerance to this.

The big trick to get a man to do just about anything is to always give him the feeling that it was *his* own decision. If he comes to the conclusion himself, he will not rebel and will stand by it.

So what was Janice to do if she wanted to spend more quality time with her guy? How could she steer him in the direction she wanted him to go? I gave her one simple assignment: "Encourage him playing golf, support him, congratulate him when he got great results. Tell him you're happy he goes out with his friends, happy that he plays golf, because that gives you the chance to (insert something that's important to you and that shows you're a high-value woman)." So that's exactly what Janice did. She became a member of an improv group, she joined a spinning class, etc.

26 days. That's exactly what it took before Mark's behavior changed. This time *he* told her, "Hey honey. What would you say if I skipped golf next Sunday and you skip your improv class so we can have lunch and spend the afternoon together?"

What should Janice have replied to this? Please stop reading and take a second to formulate your answer.

The nice girl in Janice could have responded, "Sure, great idea! Yes, I'm so happy! Sure, I'll skip class. Where will you be taking me?" **But that would have been a huge mistake**. This would prove that Janice wasn't that interested in her improv classes, that she still positioned Mark above all that, and the *only* reason she partook in those activities was because he was not available. The minute he was free, she dropped everything. This would have devalued her in Mark's eyes.

Janice luckily didn't make this mistake. I had been coaching her for a while, and she had been applying other things that you'll read in this book. Her newfound instincts helped her to immediately see what was going on:

1. Mark had given her more value.
2. Because she found other interests she was passionate about, he wanted to ditch his friends and spend time with her.
3. If she would now change her own plans, *he* would have been in control all along and would subconsciously devalue her.
4. Plus, it didn't feel right. She wasn't playing any games. She actually enjoyed improv and wanted to go (even though she, of course, wanted to spend more time with Mark too).

So here's how she replied. She said, "Great idea, Mark! However, this Sunday isn't a good fit. I'm going to go to the improv group, and then we're going out for a drink afterward. But let's take our calendars and find a time that fits us both."

They found a time and had a great date. Not long after, Mark decided to stop playing golf and be home on Sunday afternoons. *If* Janice had nothing to do, they could spend time together. Janice didn't have to nag; she didn't even have to ask him. It was all his idea...Or was it?

Men always want what they cannot have. Take something away, and he'll want it more. Increase your value, and he'll want you more.

To men, it's an effort to do anything they *have to* do relationship wise. Putting in hard work to chase you, to be with you, and treating you well when they decided to do so on their own is effortless.

Don't follow your instincts or your intuition when you want to steer a man's behavior. Do the opposite. That's how you best raise a three-year-old kid, too. If you want him to do something (or stop doing something), nagging or yelling will not work. Ignoring him always will. **Reinforce the good behavior, but ignore him whenever he shows bad behavior.**

I want to elaborate a bit here. I'm not saying that you should ignore bad behavior and just let him take you for granted or mistreat you in any way. You simply ignore him. You become less available, take longer to return his phone calls, have more important things to do than be available all the time. (You never should be available all the time anyway.)

All great men love strong women—women who won't take any crap. He will test this interestingly enough. He might and probably will give you some crap. And when he does, how you respond will define the rest of the relationship.

You'll read plenty of ways to respond throughout this book. But if you're ever in doubt, simply follow the golden rule. When a man doesn't behave the way you want, withdraw and do what you would do if you found him less important.

This always works!

If he's interested but doesn't spend enough time wi_ _ _ _ _,
withdraw. *If* he's interested, he'll want to spend more time
together. If he's late to more than one date, withdraw. If
he's interested, he'll never be late again (or at least have
the courtesy to give you a heads-up in advance).

If he says he's coming out of a difficult relationship and not
looking for anything serious, withdraw a bit and say, "Sure,
me neither. I don't know you well enough to decide if I even
want a relationship with you. We can always be friends
first and see where that goes." *If* he's interested, you'll
quickly see him get his hunting gear in order to catch you.
Make sure he never can, and he'll keep running after you
forever.

That last sentence might make you think, "All good and
well, Brian, but if he can never catch me, how on earth will I
then ever have a real relationship with him?" Simple. He
should never be able to catch and cage you.

Before I became a relationship coach, I interviewed
hundreds of couples that were together for more than ten
years and to the astonishment of their divorced friends,
were still happy. I wanted to know what their secret was.
Some had been married for over forty years. The men in
those relationships and marriages never *got* their women.
They always knew that they had to keep up their game. If
not, she might still walk away. These women never
threatened to walk. They showed them by ignoring their
husbands and withdrawing whenever their behavior was
unwanted. They always reinforced good behavior and
ignored bad behavior.

Stick to that rule and you'll never lose the interest of a man who's truly interested in the first place. Those who were just playing games, trying to get laid, trying to get your money or God knows what will disappear. And that's, although hurtful, good news.

Moreover, by ignoring him when he doesn't add value to your life and by rewarding him when he shows good behavior, you're training him just like you would a dog. And since most men are smarter than your average Labrador (some are, I've checked), it will be easy to train him.

You must never forget that a man who loves you will always love to work hard to make you happy! If he doesn't do it, that's a major red flag and a simple sign that he's not really in to you. If that's ever the case... NEXT!

We all deserve to be with someone who adores us as much as we adore them.

Predictably unpredictable

I want to lean in one other way to get him to do something. I've already mentioned that nagging never works, and I'll keep proving it throughout this book.

Nevertheless, what are you to do when you need a household chore done? Or when you just really want him to help you out with something? I've tested the strategies I'm about to give you on more than one hundred women who used them to make their boyfriends or husbands *do* something.

Let's look at the example of Rebekah, a 36-year-old woman married to a great but far from a perfect husband. There are many chores around the house William just never took care of. He's an interior designer with his own thriving company. Surely enough, this takes a lot of his time. Nevertheless, the doorknob on the bathroom door kept falling off, and Rebekah had asked William, time and time again, to fix it. She hated herself when she had to nag, but she didn't see any other way. So I asked her to stage the following: on a Sunday, when he was home, she took out the toolbox and headed up to the bathroom door where she started to make all kinds of noises with the tools. It took William less than a minute to rush in and ask, "What are you doing, honey?" Rebekah replied, "Oh nothing, I'm going to fix the doorknob." He immediately took over the tools and helped her. The door was fixed within ten minutes. No nagging needed.

What had happened here? When a man likes a woman, he likes to take care of her. He will never respond well to nagging. Nonetheless, the feeling that his wife had to take care of such a manly task made him feel less of a man, urging him to take over and fix it. Instead of nagging, just tell him you'll take care of it. Before you know it, he'll try to convince you that *he* should do it. Men...

Another great strategy used by the high-value woman is to ask *another man* to help her with something. She asks her guy to do a certain chore, twice, without nagging. He doesn't do it? Fine. "Hey John, I called my brother/colleague/friend to ask him over for dinner with his wife on Saturday. I told him about _____ that needs to get fixed, and he told me he was happy to look at it." You can bet money on it that whatever needed fixing will be fixed before Saturday.

Never underestimate a man's ego. He's governed by it. He'll do anything within his power to still believe he is *the* man. If another guy needs to take care of something for you...he isn't, he has failed.

I love these strategies because they are very effective and also help you weed out the bad men! If you don't overuse and misuse these strategies—if it doesn't become obvious why you're doing it to him—any man who still loves you, who still sees you as his woman, will go to great lengths to take care of you. If he doesn't, if he says, "Great. I'm glad that John can take care of it. I'll go out golfing with my friends" or anything similar, consider that a major red flag.

The woman every man respects and never takes for granted

I was eating out in a restaurant with my girlfriend. It was the kind of place where the tables were really close, making it impossible to not overhear other's conversations. There was a couple sitting next to us. I assume the man was in his early forties while the woman looked about thirty-five. Their conversation went something like this:

"Where do you want to go after this?" the man asked.
"I don't know. You can choose," she replied.
"No but where would you like to go?"
"Wherever you want to go," she said.

This went on for a while.

"What kind of wine would you like?" he asked.
"Whatever wine you prefer," she said.

Needless to say, it was clear this was making him more and more nervous. They finally got in a heated argument where he said, "I don't want to decide everything. It's as if I'm sitting here with a four-year-old girl." Truth be told, that was rude. But he had a point. She clearly had no opinion or will of her own, and this was making him crazy.

I guess you'd feel this exact way if you were in a relationship with a guy who always wanted to do what you want, liked what you liked, and wanted you to call *all* of the shots. Sounds great at first, but it gets boring super fast. We all prefer to be with someone with a backbone. Someone who has a clear opinion. Someone who won't always give in. This is another reason why men test women. They want you to resist them! They want you to take the lead whenever you feel like it. He wants to please you, too!

A man never takes for granted a woman with a mind of her own, her own rules, and opinions. You may be thinking, "Well duh, Brian, of course!" Question is, did you ever hide your opinion or forgot about your own rules simply to avoid making him upset? Or worse to please him? It happens to the best of us.

It's OK to please the one you love, as long as there is an equilibrium. If a woman wants to please her guy to get him to like her more, there is, by definition, no equilibrium. She's doing it for all of the wrong reasons.

There's a strange insight about men that I want to give you. Men love to work hard to get and help a woman they like (this final part being the crucial part). It's been engrained in their instincts to want to take care of their woman. However, men hate it when a woman doesn't hold her own, when she becomes dependent on him. Not financially, of course, but emotionally. He wants to know what you're passionate about, what makes you tick, and what makes you love life. That's why any man quickly gets bored of the nice girl who makes her life revolve around him.

The more you *need* him, the less he will want you. The more you *want* him, the more he will need you.

A strong independent woman wants a man. A sweet, soft, nice girl needs a man; she feels incomplete without one. If this happens to be how you feel, you have two options.

1. Don't show him you need him. Partake in extra activities just to make sure that he cannot and will not become the center of your life.
2. Work on your mental strength. Whenever you feel the "I need him" trap coming closer, consciously decide what's happening and tell yourself this is a self-fulfilling prophecy. The more you try not to lose him because you need him, the higher the probability he will eventually leave just because of this.

Always be prepared to walk away and make him know and feel this. You can keep using the "ignore him and withdraw when he's bad and love him when he's good" attitude. This will send a very clear message to him.

And just in case he still doesn't get it, be assertive! Say, "You must have mistaken me for one of those women who puts up with this crap. I won't."

The high-value woman always keeps him guessing.

He never knows where he really stands with her. He knows she likes him, of course, she doesn't hide it, but he never knows how much. She doesn't throw I love yous around. He never knows when he'll have sex with her again. Nothing ever is solely on *his* terms. Both he and she are equal in the relationship, with often a little bit more power to her. She keeps him on his toes and makes sure there's always a bit or mystery, regardless of how many decades they've already been together.

Using a man's ego to help him see things YOUR way

Men are governed by their egos. It's their primary motivator. Dumb men are *only* ruled by their ego. Say something that hurts their ego and they will erupt in anger or tears. Smarter men are a bit more emotionally intelligent and try to decide whether an emotion is valid or not. Nonetheless, they still need to manage all those emotions their egos give to them.

It will come as no surprise, but men like to feel important. The more important you are to a man, the more it will matter that *you* show how important he is to you. Besides sex, this is your second most important weapon! Play his ego right and he will behave like a cute puppy while *he* thinks he is in control (this is important to his ego).

Let me be blunt. Most women are looking for security. You might be the exception that confirms the rule, but most women are designed to look for a great guy and then make sure he stays with them forever. Men are different. They are looking for power. That's their number one priority.

Think about it. How many women did you ever see end up in jail because of fraud or setting up a Ponzi scheme (like Bernard Madoff). A Ponzi scheme is designed to fail from the start. Just in case you haven't heard of a Ponzi scheme, here's how this works.

Mr. Fraud opens an investment firm and says, "Give me your money, and I'll give you an interest rate of 10 percent (a number that's clearly higher than the current market rates)." Mr. Ibelieveinfairytales is hesitant and skeptical, so he says, "Here, I'll give you $10,000 to see how that goes."

Over the next few months, Mr. Fraud finds a lot of Ibelieveinfairytales men and women and rakes in $200,000. He goes back to the first investor and says, "Here is $11,000 back. Your initial $10,000 plus 10 percent." That money simply came from the other dreamers. He uses their money to pay back his first investors.

Ibelieveinfairytales thinks to himself, "Wow! That actually worked. Mr. Fraud is not a fraudster or a liar; he clearly must know what he's doing. I'm going to give him $100,000 now so he can do the same with it. YES! I'm going to be rich soon." And he does. Mr. Fraud now uses that money to give the other dreamers their money back plus interest, a lot of them are in awe and invest even more because they too see the dollar signs.

This system, a Ponzi scheme, works great...until it no longer does. Then it falls down like a house of cards. Mr. Fraud can live a lavish lifestyle and swim in money. But since he never invested any of the money, he's losing money from the start. He can only keep paying people back as long as new people keep investing (since he always uses that money to pay back earlier investors). When the market crashes, or when anything happens in the world that makes new investors hold on to their money or worse, people ask for their money back, his system fails. This will always happen at some point, of course. Mr. Fraud is then sent to jail. I never got this. Ponzi schemes always fail eventually. So why do so many people try to set them up? Because they are addicted to money and the power it brings.

Why are there generally no women *that* stupid to set up a Ponzi scheme? Because they are not, in general, blindly and stupidly driven by power. Most men will do almost anything if they believe it will give them more power.

ALL men are driven by their ego. And if you use this wisely, you can drive men.

I admit I'm no different. When my long-time girlfriend states something as a fact, my instinct is to always say, "No, in fact..." and then to try and prove her wrong. That's my ego talking. I, of course, overrule it and really listen to what my loving girlfriend has to say. But still, the instinct is there; my ego is always trying to be right. I cannot change it. I can overrule it, but the basic instinct is there, in all men.

You can use this to your advantage. All you need is some reverse psychology. This is not playing a game by the way; it's simply using the knowledge you have about what works best on men.

Let me give you an example. You're used to your car going to the left when you turn the steering wheel to the left. If I'd give you a car where this is inversed, it would take you a day or two and you'd be driving around like nothing happened.

Men are to be treated like this. Most of what makes them tick makes no sense at all and is the exact opposite of what it should be. Simply accept this and use it. If you want your guy to stay home more often, tell him to go out more! If you want your man to clean up his mess more often, don't clean it up for him, don't nag, don't even say anything about it. Just drop your mess on top of his, make the place even messier, and before you know it, *he* will be the one saying to clean up more...and he'll do it too! If you want your boyfriend to text you more, text him less. If you want your man to appreciate you cooking for him, cook less for him or cook him some really simple meals. If you're dating a guy and you want to go steady with him, tell him you're not sure he's the right guy to date. **In short, do the exact opposite of what would make sense.**

There are two reasons why this works. First, the challenge builds up. I've already discussed to great extent why giving a man a challenge works so well. It's like throwing a stick for a dog; he can't help but run after it. Second, he'll think all of this is HIS decision, just the way his ego likes it. A man will for instance never ask a woman to marry him until he believes it was *his* decision. His fragile ego wouldn't be able to live with itself knowing he got trapped into a marriage. His ego doesn't want to be told what to do.

So if you want him to do something, tell him not do to it. Childish, abysmal, totally ridiculous? I know. But that's the way we, men, function. And it's good for you, the woman. Once you get his basic functioning, it will be easy to steer him into any direction you want.

My girlfriend is really good at this!

When we were about to move in together, I got a rush of commitment fear. We were packing up her belongings in her then apartment. I had been a bachelor all of my life, going from one adventure to the next. So my ego realized my life was over and was never ever going to be the same again. (Silly ego. My life is much better now.) My girlfriend, the high-value woman she is, noticed my fear and said, "Don't worry. I'm not putting a ball and chains on your ankles; you can throw me out whenever you want." My fear dissipated faster than snow would melt in the Las Vegas desert.

What had happened here? Remember the inverted steering wheel? My girlfriend used it.

Her logical response would have been, "I see fear in your eyes. Do you still love me? Where is this going? I don't want to be wasting my time here. We're going to get married eventually, right?" This would have made my ego so scared that I might not have been able to overrule it. But she knew that to get what she wanted, she had to steer in the opposite and illogical direction. She gave my ego control. I thought, "Aha! So I can throw her out whenever I want? Then there must be no risk. I do like her a lot, so there's no need to worry." And my ego (and I) behaved exactly the way she wanted.

The lesson here is: don't always say what you want him to hear. Say what he **needs** to hear to do what you want! My ego thought it was in control. Yet, *she* had been the one with the power all along! Reverse psychology works well on three-year-old boys, and it continues to work well on men of all ages.

I once interviewed a high-value woman who was really good at this. Whenever she wanted something done, she gave her guy a couple of options. She would say, "Honey, what do you prefer? Do you want to go to the park on Sunday, or would you rather visit that new exhibition in town?" His ego was happy. It thought it was in control and got to choose. But both options were of course fine for our high-value woman in this example. And if she really wanted to lead him into one direction, she just chose an option that she knew *he* wouldn't like. "Hey honey, quick question: Would you rather have me vacuum the living room on Sunday (while he'll be watching the game) or do *you* have time to do it on Saturday?"

Guess what he'll pick? And the funny thing is, his ego will love it! It got to be in control...so it believes.

Clearly, you'll need to pick your battles. You can't use these strategies every single day. He'll be on to you if you do and then it will lose its power. Use his ego whenever it's *really* important to you that he does something. And remember the golden rule since this one will always work: reinforce good behavior, and ignore bad behavior.

This doesn't mean you should accept any bad behavior or lack of good behavior!

I hope it's clear I want you to have the power, or share the power with him. The trick is, every now and then, he'll need to feel like he's the king and able to rule over his country, make certain decisions, and feel important. His queen is softer, more feminine, and uses an emotionally intelligent way to get the king to do what she wants. That's the problem with women who nag or complain. It makes their boyfriends feel like crap.

Let's look at a scenario.

Katie wants her guy to do more of the chores in the household (taking out the trash, filling and emptying the dishwasher, buying her flowers, preparing some meals, etc.). She has the option to nag, "Why don't you ever cook for us? Why don't you empty the dishwasher? Why am I always the one who _____?" This might work in the short term, but it never ever will work in the long term.

Katie's boyfriend will feel like a loser because she continuously tells him he is! He's not good enough for her, clearly. That's what his ego will conclude. Can you blame it? She's always talking down to it. He never does anything right.

Katie, however, also has another option. One night he *does* take out the trash. When he walks back into the house she says, "I love it when you take out the trash." After he cooked something (even though he really has to learn how to combine flavors) she says, "It was a delicious meal. I love it when a man knows how to cook." You guessed it. These are ego-strokes. Like a puppy, every man's ego loves to be stroked...and wants more of it.

As a result, his ego will think, "hmmm...let's take out the trash more!" or "Let's look up some recipes online and try to impress her even more the next time." You may think I'm kidding, but I'm not. This works! Many studies have been done to confirm this. Harvard Business Review wrote an article[2] stating that the ideal praise to criticism ratio in relationships is 5 to 1—five positive comments for every negative one. John Gottman, the famous researcher from the Gottman Institute who started studying couples in the 1970s in his research lab, found that for people who end up in divorce, the ratio is 0.77 to 1. This means three positive comments for every four negative ones.[3]

Nagging is the worst way to get a man to do anything, and *the* best way to push a relationship over the cliff. If he does anything you don't like or refrains from doing stuff you like, you should never ever simply accept it. You deserve the best!

Nevertheless, don't nag or complain to get it. Reinforce good behavior and or ignore him when he shows bad behavior. Ignoring his ego (by ignoring him) will hurt and work much better than complaining.

---

[2] Harvard Business Review, 2013/03 The ideal Praise to criticism
[3] Gottman, J.M. and Levenson, R. 1999

His ego wants to be in your good graces. It wants to protect you, care for you, and be your man. When a man loves you, all he wants to do is to protect and to serve. Let him.

One important remark, don't overdo it! Anything available in abundance loses all of its value. Never over-compliment him. Spoon-feed your ego strokes and compliments, so it always remains a challenge to get them. He has to earn them. *He wants to earn them!*

Quickly train him to be a good boy

I'm not sure what camp you belong to, but I've seen my fair share of feministas. These were women who wanted to split the bill after the first date, got annoyed when you open a door for them or pull out a chair, and wanted to take care of the heavy lifting in the house because "women can do this too, you know." Well of course they can! No sane man will ever deny this! But here's the challenge these women fail to see. If you don't let him help in the early stages where you literally set the stage, why would he do it later on?

You'll need to trigger his "I want to take care of my woman" instincts from the very beginning. This is necessary for three reasons:

1. He needs it! He cares for the woman he loves. And he loves the woman he cares for! For the love of you, allow him to care for you.

2. This is potty training your guy. If and when he learns to put in an effort from the get-go, he won't mind doing it 5 to 65 years down the line.

3. This is a great filter to weed out the bad guys. Guys who play games or who are in any way not really interested in you will only do the bare minimum to still get what they want. This could be sex, often, but it can also mean getting a home cooked meal every night or anything else you do for him. The more effort you see him put into you and the relationship, the more he really likes you...regardless of what he says! A guy who says "I'm not ready for a real commitment," but mows your lawn, takes out your trash, fixes your tire, pays for the dates, or makes life easier for you is a far better catch than a guy who says "I see us getting married someday" but doesn't put in any effort. Words are cheap; actions are priceless. The high-value woman knows this very well. She doesn't see it as her losing control when he says "step aside honey, let me fix this." She considers it a job well done!

The probation period

The high-value woman lets every man she considers for a long-term relationship go through an extensive probation period. Even though her primal instincts and oxytocin levels might be screaming, "Latch on and NEVER let this guy go! He's the one! He really is. YES, you found him. Your worries are over. You'll be all right. From now on, the sun will shine every day. Just don't let him go. You'll never ever find another man, especially not a great guy like this one. I mean, it *feels* so right, doesn't it? So it MUST be that he is the one!" The high-value woman looks at this for what it is: the love radio station. She rarely tunes in because she knows her emotions are untrustworthy.

Every single guy, even "the one," needs to go through a probation period. She wants to get to know him *well*. The high-value woman knows every man will show his best game early in the relationship. She wants to sit that part out before she makes up her mind. She also wants to see how he behaves when life is not treating him well, when he's let go at work, when he's sick, when he loses out on an important contract, when the waiter brings him the wrong dish, when his car has been scratched in the parking lot, etc. She wants to observe him and get to know him well.

And here's the trick. She observes. She keeps quiet about what she sees.

If he does a no-no, she takes notes. She won't complain, nag, or get mad. She wouldn't want him to change his behavior *just* because she got mad, just because he wants to avoid a fight.

In case this needs a bit of explaining, men hate fights. They prefer to have their arm bitten off by a hungry alligator with smelly breath than to get in yet another fight that makes no sense to them (it never does). Many studies have been done around this subject, especially by the Gottman Institute. We don't need studies, however. Every woman who has ever had a fight with a man knows that men cannot handle the emotions that erupt during a fight. They might seem to not care on the surface, but studies show their physiological reactions (heart rate, sweat, etc.) not only go up but stay elevated for hours after the fight has been over.

Since no sane man likes these feelings, he'll go through great lengths to avoid them. This includes hiding the fact that he started smoking again, hiding the fact that naked porn stars seem to have found the hard drive of his computer again, even though he promised to never ever do these things again.

That's one of the many reasons why nagging is not a good idea. Nevertheless, the high-value woman wants to see how he behaves in his natural habitat, when he thinks no one is judging him. She wants to make sure she gets to know the *real* him as quickly as possible. The real him is the guy who will always resurface later in the relationship anyway, so she wants to make sure she loves *that* part of him too.

When his report card has too many bad points, she's out of there. She doesn't ask him to change, complain, or wait it out. She knows he won't change.

The high-value woman slows *him* down

Remember Jamie? She's the 57-year-old woman who found her knight in shining armor. He asked her to marry her after a couple of months and then ran for the hills a while later, calling off the wedding and disappearing forever.

The high-value woman knows men cannot handle emotions very well. She knows this probation period is an absolute must for him too! Even when *he* falls head over heels and wants to go fast, even then (especially then!), she paces herself and explains they need to take things slowly. She wants to learn who he is first and give him the time to get to know her well too.

More importantly, as explained before, she guards her own life and passions. If she would jump on board and allow herself to get drifted away by the passion that a new relationship brings, she will lose herself. It will be way too easy for her to become needy, to put all of her eggs into his basket, and to start depending on him.

Unlike him, *she* does think ahead.

Before meeting her prince, the high-value woman had her life pretty well in order. She had her career, hobbies, passions, social activities, habits, etc. She knows she should never ever throw those out right away just because she met a great guy, regardless of how nice, respectful, or affectionate he is toward her.

I want to stress this. The high-value woman doesn't give up on her life to get some attention from the bad boy she met. She doesn't adapt to his agenda. On the other hand, she won't adapt to the nicest man in the world who truly loves her either! She doesn't want to lose her stability, her habits, her life.

Even if she's dealing with a great guy who clears his entire agenda to be with her as much as he can, she won't allow him! She has built up her life before him, and she's adamant about not throwing that away.

This is tough.

The high-value woman is not a robot. She's human, after all. She can be flooded by feelings and butterflies. Her body might be screaming that she should spend every second with her love interest, especially because he wants it too! He keeps asking her out!

Nonetheless, she uses her emotional intelligence and thinks long term. So she limits the early stages to two or three dates per week. She declines the other attempts to get together. She continues her yoga class, her favorite TV show, her evening walks, and most of what was important to her before meeting *him.* She consciously decides to not throw her own life overboard, even when all the lights are green and it seems like this guy *is* the one.

Fighting this urge to be with him is not easy. But believe me, it's way easier than all the heartache that would follow if she'd rush in.

When a man wants to go fast, she controls the rhythm since she doesn't want him to hurt himself *and* her in the process. She knows that when she allows him to run, he will outrun himself, fall down, get scared, and stop seeing her. When she paces him, his fear of commitment won't surface.

Why great men are so difficult to attract and keep

Great men are in short supply. If we weed out all the bad types of men, like the players, narcissists, overly nice guys, perverts, psychopaths, losers, mommy boys... there are not a lot of men left.

Like you, other women have a nose for these great guys. This gives these men the power of choice. You'll need to compete with other women. Something you might not even want to do in the first place! You're not doing yourself any favors. You *should* compete. You're worth it. You deserve the best type of love life you can get. And nothing that's worth having is ever effortless.

It's not a fight, mind you. It's not a real competition. It's never the woman who's overtly fighting for attention who gets the great guy. This is by definition a low-value woman in their opinion. Competing, in this case, means being more laid back and putting in *less* of an effort! Not more.

These great men fall for confident women. Confidence is a word that covers a lot of ground. There's not just one type of confidence. Confidence means knowing you have a certain area of your life fully under control. So you could be very confident in the fact that you know how to cook well and then have no confidence at all when it comes to walking up to a guy or knowing what to say during the first date.

There's no need for you to be confident in every area of your life. Nobody is anyway.

You're not perfect, and that's perfect!

You've heard me explain how the high-value woman thinks and acts. I have been and will be painting the ideal picture. You're not perfect, and she's not perfect. Nobody is. That's OK! We can only do the best we can with what we've got. Please do not feel bad if you realize you've not acted like a high-value woman at certain times in the past. That's normal. The high-value woman I describe wasn't born like this. She too has had to learn and develop certain qualities that allow her to protect her heart and at the same time be open to a great and fulfilling relationship with a high-quality guy.

The goal is that you install a little virtual bell so whenever a man does something funny, disrespectful, or illogical in any way, before reacting you say, "How would a high-value woman respond?" You'll be surprised with the results.

The high-value woman's most important quality

The most important quality of every high-value woman is a strong set of boundaries. She will always value herself more than *any* guy...no matter how great she believes he is, no matter how much she's in love with him. This is why it needs to be a quality she possesses. Just like anyone else, she too will be blinded by love every now and then. As a guy disrespects her, she might think, "He probably didn't mean it, he will change. I'll give him another chance." Then her quality kicks in, and she thinks, "No, no. I choose me first. I need to enforce my boundaries. Even though I prefer not to lose him, *this* behavior is unacceptable. I'll assertively state my needs. If he then makes that same mistake again, he's out!"

Ignore him and withdraw whenever he does something you don't like. If, however, he does something truly disrespectful, you should always state it and show you are ready to walk away, without bluffing...even after thirty-five years of marriage.

The high-value woman doesn't ever let men have their way with *her* emotions, time, body, money, or career. And this is a boundary she strongly protects. Every boundary she bends or changes is only changed when he deserved it. It's never given.

When a high-value woman is in a relationship with a high-value guy, they behave like a team. They both make concessions, but there's always an equilibrium. Not a quid pro quo where every concession from her needs to be met by a concession from him. The relationship is always a win-

win. Never a lose-win or even a win-lose. (She doesn't want to dominate her guy either.)

The high-value woman can get blinded by love, too. But she has previously built in the habit to enforce her boundaries and to stick to her rulebook, even though it might not feel like the right thing to do at the time. One of her rules, for instance, is: "I will only invest myself as much in the relationship as he invests himself in it." This is a habit she has. When a guy she's with starts to lose interest, she won't start to invest more (even though her instinct will want to make her run harder after him). She plays by her rules and doesn't let them get clouded by her emotions.

Your emotions are never to be trusted. Countless times you've had fear, anger, or other negative emotions when they were not needed. I come from a background of panic attacks (I had them for fourteen years while growing up), so I know from firsthand experience how untrustworthy our emotions can be. If you let them rule your life, you'll be living a severely limited life.

Her tolerance level doesn't change. There are no excuses. Excuses like "He just got out of a difficult relationship, that's why he's behaving like this" or "He has a lot of stuff going on at work" or "He promised me he would change" have no meaning to her even though these thoughts might pop up.

You know the funny part about this quality? Her strong personal boundaries protect her from getting played and work as a magnet to attract great guys.

Players don't like to play games. Silly as that sounds, players, narcissists, and most types of bad men search for weak prey—a woman they can control with the smallest possible investment from their side. They will not stick around the high-value woman because she's too high maintenance for them. Good for them. They're weeding themselves out.

High-quality men, however, love to work hard for what is dear to them. They don't mind making a major investment. That's the way they've been living their lives for a very long time. They didn't become great guys by choosing the easy road. So meeting a woman who has high standards only makes them more attracted to her. They love women who have strong personal boundaries and are confident enough to know what they want and demand it. High-quality men always respect women who do not tolerate manipulative games and have solid standards. Those standards need to be realistic, of course. Some women have impossible standards.

Both high- and low-value women attract losers and bad men. The difference is a low-value woman will stick around and wait it out, hoping he will change...or worse, thinking this is the best she can get. She will accept his disinterest or his constantly fluctuating interest.

Avoid Getting Played

Players, narcissists, bad boys, manipulators, douchebags, losers...all seek out women who are weak. Women they *can* play and manipulate.

Many of the women I coach ask, "Why do I always attract jerks?" Every woman attracts jerks! The difference is high-quality women don't stay with a jerk; they don't keep dating him. So there's nothing wrong with you attracting jerks. You're an attractive woman, so you'll attract all kinds of men! A hot flame attracts butterflies too, not just moths. The question is, who are the men you'll keep around?

Weak women—to be absolutely clear, I don't consider you one of them since weak women don't read books like these to learn and improve their skills—are needy and accept bad behavior because they believe that's all they can get. "It's better than being alone," they figure. All types of bad men prey on that very belief.

Players and bad men will base themselves on their first impression of you. And great guys will obviously also be attracted because of the first impression. Your first impression on men is built up on two stages:

1. Your looks

    Men are attracted to good-looking women. So it's normal that you'd spend at least some time making sure you'll make the right impression in the looks department.

    That said, the man you're in a long-term relationship with will eventually get used to your looks. Plus, there are plenty of other pretty women out there. Women who only use their looks to get men find it harder to differentiate themselves from other women and cannot prevent men from becoming indifferent after a couple of weeks, months, or years. There's always a prettier and younger version out there.

Your personality, the way you make him feel, *that's* the true differentiator! That's what makes you unique.

2. Your personality. **This is the most important part.**

   Most women spend the least amount of attention on this part of a first impression. They spend a lot of time wondering "how do I look?" and less time on "how do I act?" This is where the high-value woman makes the difference. She understands her personality is her main differentiator. That's why you'll see many average- or even bad-looking high-value women with great guys who adore them. Great guys know they need to look far beyond your looks.

Just like high-quality men are in short supply, so are high-value women. I'm sure you've seen this in social gatherings. The more you act and behave like a high-value woman, your power of choice increases. Not just romantically. High-value women get better jobs, higher salaries, better everything.

When you first meet a guy, he has already noticed your looks a long time before. Your personality, however, is something he'll start to base upon your behavior and on what you say (and don't say). I've discussed what not to do in my other books like *Are You Scaring Him Away?* and *21 Traps*. Here I'll discuss what *to* do and how the high-value woman handles it.

I'm sure I'm not the first person to tell you how important first impressions are. They really are! We all suffer from some kind of cognitive filter in our brain that sticks to the first image we get. That's a cognitive distortion often called the first impression bias. As soon as we have created our first impression we set it in stone and start filtering out everything that proves our impression was right. All of the evidence against our first impression is automatically discarded.

Our brains do this to save energy. Since our brains use up a ton of energy, they have a lot of shortcuts to avoid using processing power whenever it's not necessary. When you see a car, your brain doesn't look back at that car to second-guess whether you were right or not. If it looks like a car, it *is* a car. We can make misjudgments because of this.

Did you ever meet someone at work who made a bad first impression? This person said or did something that you did not like at all. Your first impression has been created. Then, days or even weeks later you enter a meeting room and guess who sits at the meeting table? *That* person. Your mind will immediately come up with the bad feeling that has been linked to that specific person, and this will strongly influence how you will respond to that person. A wasp only needed to sting you once for you to never ever forget those nasty little creatures are not to be trusted.

So this is a cognitive distortion we all have and need. If you're ever walking around in the jungle and you see a tiger in front of you, your feelings of danger will start to increase right away. You won't get the time to second-guess your first impression and think, "Well, he looks cute and not so hungry...he resembles that tiger from Winnie the Pooh and that was a kind tiger. Will this one be kind too? Should I check it out?" This type of thinking would obviously get you injured or worse, killed. Long story short, our minds tend to stick to our first impression. This is yet another primal instinct.

This has both negative and positive consequences. If you mess up the first impression, you can virtually forget it. It will take a long time to reset it. On the other hand, if you make a great first impression, you have a lot of room to drop the ball here and there afterwards. Here, too, it will take a long time before the first impression will change.

That's why you'll need to work hard on the first impression you make, especially on men. Men decide within the first couple of minutes whether they see you as long-term girlfriend or wife material. When a woman makes the wrong first impression, you'll see that her boyfriend needs a lot more time before he's able to commit. That's because he wants to wait and see which way the wind blows. He needs time to prove his first impression wrong (men with real commitment issues aside).

Here are some strategies that will help you make a good first impression.

Your attention doesn't come cheap

Ah, love! There's nothing better than meeting someone who sparks all the butterflies in your stomach with a single look or a single date. When this happens, it feels like you've finally found the path to happily ever after. Only, fairy tales are just that, fairy tales. As much as we all like to feel like a teenager in love again, it can be disastrous to your love life when you do it too soon. There is a time and place for intoxicating romance, but that time is rarely in the very beginning of the encounter.

Even though you'd love nothing more than to spend all of your attention on Mr. Right, you'll need to keep dosing it well until *he* has proven his worth. Be as eager as he is, never more. He should always be the one chasing you and showing his interest in you, not the other way around.

Some women make mistakes here. They're so happy to be in love that they lavish their new guy with attention, affection, and love. He doesn't deserve this yet. Most men, especially great men, will consider this desperate behavior. It is. It stems from some kind of anxiety where these women think, "Oh, finally! A great guy. I must latch and hold on to him forever. Let me crush him with my love to prove to him what I'm worth." This will indeed crush him, and he will run away. For some women, this behavior stems from a fear of never finding a great man and when one then finally comes along, he must not be lost. These women place *that* much value on him that they totally devalue themselves. This very anxiety will spread on to him. I have yet to meet a guy who can live with this burden. He needs to know he has worked for your love and attention. What is given too soon and freely seems cheap. Your love and attention are not cheap. So be careful on whom you spend it.

High-value women know what they are worth. They'd rather be single than in a relationship with the wrong kind of guy. They spoon-feed their attention to guys who haven't proven their worth yet. And when I talk about worth, I never mean financially. I'm talking about courteous behavior, respect, and most importantly, authenticity.

High-quality men want to fight for your attention. This is a tricky one. Some women know this and then try to make a man jealous by openly flirting with other men. This might work on low-quality men with fragile egos, but high-quality men see right through this ploy and consider it needy behavior. It's a different fight they need and like.

Consider this. You meet a great guy, and *you* have started the conversation. After only 5-7 minutes, you say, "It was nice talking to you. I've got to go back to...(work/my friends/someone else)." You've just increased your value considerably. You clearly are a woman who has a lot going on in her life. You don't clinch onto the first guy you meet. If he wants more of you, he'll have to fight for it.

This is a very strong high-quality signal that can significantly increase the quality of the first impression you've made. If you meet someone, even though you'd like to spend the next 100 years by his side, be gone after a couple of minutes. You can always come back later. That, or he can run after you, which is even better.

Were you ever approached by a guy who introduced himself and then just hung around? You just couldn't get rid of him. That clingy behavior will make you uncomfortable within minutes. The most important people, during any networking event, move around from one group to another. If they're not the organizer, they behave like one, introducing themselves here and there, asking a couple of interesting questions, and moving around the room. They then go back to the people they found really interesting, the people who earned their attention. If you use this strategy on men, you'll significantly raise your value.

Always make them earn your attention. From the very first second they meet you until long after "I do."

The more important and high quality the man is, the *more* he should earn your attention. There's an important strategy behind this. Picture a great guy. He's good-looking, smart, and athletic. Ever since he turned 16, he's been getting more attention from women than his male friends, who obviously envy him. He was the guy who always got the best-looking girlfriends. Some of these guys then turn into obnoxious bad boys who deserve to be in dating hell. Don't worry. They eventually get there. A smaller group of these lucky men stay gentlemen. They are a rare breed, and they know it. They get attention from women here and there and get many offers. After their first relationship experiences, they start to become picky, because they can. As they meet women, they feel they could get seven out of every ten women they meet. These are, however, not the women they want. They wonder why the three women they seemingly have no powers over are different. These are the women they are interested in and want to get to know better.

This doesn't mean you cannot initiate contact. It *does* mean the better the guy you're interested in is, the more it becomes important to let the guy do the chasing. Great men have enough women throwing themselves at their feet. The high-value woman is different. You are high value and can be picky too. He will sense that, and that's what will trigger his initial attraction level.

So how do you show this to him quickly?

Your time is one of your most valuable assets. Time is the only thing we can never buy more of. The clock keeps ticking, so what you spend your time on is important; it's like a vote. You vote something as important by spending time on it. Only start to chip away time normally spent with friends, family, your hobbies, even your pets when he *really* deserves it. Always spoon-feed your attention and your time in the beginning. That will be crucial if you want to create a great first impression.

Don't give up your hobbies, leisure, anything. I've coached so many women who skip yoga class, tennis, cooking class, and more just to spend time with a guy who doesn't deserve it yet. Make him work for your time first!

Crucially, this also means you are not the one who *keeps* initiating contact. It's OK to initiate the first contact, but then it's up to him. A lot of women make mistakes here. They believe, "Well, we're no longer living in the fifties. Why would a woman not be able to get in touch with a guy whenever and however much she pleases?" I get it. Like I always say, women are equal to men (if not better than men), but men and women are not alike. There are certain rules that govern the way attraction works. You can fight those rules, but your love life will probably suffer the consequences. When you keep initiating contact, your attention becomes cheap. It's freely available. He doesn't have to work for it. You might as well hang a sign around your neck that says, "Grab and go!" And we both know you're not like that, but *he* won't!

The biggest reason, in my opinion, why your attention should never come cheap is because it will automatically weed out the bad men. I think you will agree when I say that the guy who deserves to be in a long-term relationship with you should be someone who doesn't take you for granted, who fought for you, and who gladly has put in the time and effort required to get you. The men who do this will never be ambivalent. You'll never have to wonder,

"Does he like me? Does he like me not?" This strategy will automatically weed out the doubters or men with other issues.

You don't need saving

Men are afraid of women who need to be saved. These are women who currently are in a bad relationship or women who are unhappily single. Needless to say, the high-value woman never stays in an unhappy relationship. She has better things to do with her time than to wait around for a guy to get his act together. She prefers to be single. And when she is single, she enjoys it. Her life is never solely built around "finding a man who will love me." She has the urge to find a great guy. We all want someone to share our lives with. It's programmed into our DNA. But even when she's in a relationship, her guy will never be the center of her life.

And that's the crucial part. Men are afraid of women who make *them* the center of their lives, their only source of true happiness. Unhappy singles signal this quality to the men they meet. Lower quality men might look this over because *they* are happy to get some attention too. The high-quality men, however, can be picky and will not forgo this.

Although looks are important to most men, any great guy will always pick a less good-looking woman who's confident, content, and full of self-love over the needy but super attractive bombshell.

Don't crave his attention

Your attention doesn't come cheap. Getting his attention shouldn't be too valuable at first. When I look at the list of women I've coached over the years, a large portion of them made the mistake of seeking the attention, the approval, or even the love of the men they'd just met. This is an easy way to signal needy behavior to men. Even when you are not needy at all!

I get it. We all want to feel important and get some love. Receiving attention from someone we're attracted to feels better than almost anything in this world. Yet this is exactly where high-value women make the difference and *earn* their value. His attention doesn't mean anything to them, at first, since he has not proven to be worthy or high value himself. This is not something he can prove with his looks or a couple of hours of conversation. It takes a long series of dates and seeing how he responds in a variety of situations for him to build up the value she accords to him.

Always travel light

Men are afraid of women with baggage. They won't mind carrying a ton of your luggage later on, but if they see you *arrive* with baggage, most men will run, especially the great guys (again, because they can be picky).

As he's forming his first impression of you, it's best to stay away from anything that's negative. If he's a great guy, he will too. We all have our scars and problems from the past, but that doesn't mean we should showcase them too soon.

This means:
- Not talking about bad experiences with men in general or previous boyfriends
- Not complaining about anything at all (even though we all have stuff to complain about)
- Not talking about what problems we faced during our childhood

- Do talk about what's going great in life. What passion projects are you working on? What's going well? What are you happy about?

Self-respect, your number one ally

If you want to create a great first impression, never do anything that would prove you have no self-respect. I'll dig into the details later, but in short, this means that you will never adapt or change your behavior to please anyone or worse, to get attention or love from anyone.

Men who sense that you have a lot of self-respect will immediately position you very high on the value ladder. They can only find out you have *it* when you show it. Lower the value and attention you give him whenever he does something that shows indifference or disrespect.

Playing hard to get is the worst thing you can do

The high-value woman never plays hard to get. She never plays games at all. If the need to play games would ever arise, she simply withdraws. She will never ever fight for his attention; it should be the other way around. Men should be and will be fighting for *your* attention.

Playing hard to get is still trying to get his attention. That's the main difference. The high-quality woman will only give her attention to the men fighting for hers. She, of course, has a trick or two up her sleeve to make him fight for her.

The high-value woman *is* hard to get. She doesn't need to play it. She doesn't need to consciously map it out as a strategy. She only sparingly gives her time and attention to the men who work for it, the men putting in the necessary efforts.

A good relationship can never be built upon games, unless you don't mind playing games for the rest of your life. Some women pick this path, but if you ask me, it's a bad one. It results in major insecurities and will make your relationship the main worry in your life, all the time. If that's the case, how on earth could you then build your career, friendships, and more when a guy keeps sucking away all of your brain power?

Weeding the bad from the good men

Bad men have a tendency to limit their investment in the women they're with. That's the red line that links all of the types of bad men together.

Here are two quick examples. Losers will text you to keep in touch. Great guys might be less communicative (since they are busy), but when they do get in touch, they'll pick up the phone, actually dial your number, and spend time talking to you. This is a different investment, isn't it?

Low-quality men will cancel dates, change plans, or call for a last-minute get-together. They don't value your time. High-quality men value their time *and* yours. When they set a date, it's as important as everything else in their calendar. They wouldn't think about canceling it. They also rarely call for last-minute get-togethers since they know and assume you have important things to do as well. They presume you're not waiting around for them to call.

That's what high-value women play into. They force this behavior upon the men they meet. Losers and bad men will quickly dismiss themselves; they won't be able to stick by those rules. Good men wouldn't want it any other way. Most often this rule will not even have to be enforced. And just in case it has, the high-value woman will say something to the tune of, "I think you have me mistaken for another type of woman. I don't like men who (fill in what you dislike)." This is not nagging; this is simply stating a fact.

How to use self-respect to attract great men

Your most powerful asset is not, contrary to popular belief, your bosom or your sexy behind. I know it's hard to imagine men who can look beyond the physical attributes of a woman. These men are out there, but I admit, they are in short supply.

All kidding aside, your most powerful asset is your self-respect. If you take an introspective look at yourself, you may ask how much do you adapt or even change your behavior to get someone's approval? This is a mistake I used to make a lot in the past. So many people (the old me included) waste so much time on trying to be liked or on trying to change the behavior of other people.

Let's continue to be vulnerable and honest. How many times did you get mad, nag, or complain because you wanted someone else to change his or her behavior? Did it work in the long term?

It never does.

When you adapt your behavior to get anything from anyone, you are setting your self-respect aside. And yet your self-respect is your most attractive trait. It's one that will never age or fade as long as you *choose* to keep it intact.

Let's look at the average woman as an example. She's been in a relationship with a guy for two months. They're not living together. She keeps bringing up the subject of moving in but whenever she does, he withdraws and starts to stonewall her. He also doesn't always return her phone calls and has other flaky behavior.

Can you get what our average woman will do in an attempt to change his behavior?

She will:

- A. Nag
- B. Get mad
- C. Complain
- D. Keep bringing it up
- E. All of the above

You've guessed it. The correct answer is E. She will do all of the above. Most probably not all at the same time, yet she will try different variations of nagging, getting mad, complaining, and she will definitely keep bringing it up.

OK. How would the high-value woman respond in this exact situation?

- A. She will give him less attention.
- B. She will start seeing him less.
- C. She will not go out of her way to cater his needs.
- D. She will spend more time on her hobbies, seeing her friends and family, etc.
- E. All of the above

Yes, you are good! I know you've guessed it. It's E again. It seems so simple and yet this is a mistake that's easily made.

Here's why that is. We, humans, do not like change. We resent it and would love for everything to stay just the way it is (unless it's bad, of course). How do *you* deal with change?

When we're in a relationship with someone, we're happy we've found someone to love, someone who hopefully loves us back, and someone we can have a good time with. If that person then doesn't seem right for us or starts to display behavior we dislike, the rational solution would be to dump that person straight away. NEXT!

However, that would represent a massive change. It would mean breaking up with that guy, going through the hardship of that breakup, and then being single...again. Who knows when the next great guy will come along, if ever.

These might be thoughts you then have. They are nevertheless nothing more than your negative voice that will always keep yapping negative stuff in your ear. We all have it and what it says is often a simple distortion. Some women, however, do listen and then figure. "If I could just get him to pay more attention to me, to move in with me, to...". That sounds like the path with the least change and thus the least resistance. Question is, is it really?

This is where the high-value woman makes the difference and why she, in fact, *is* high value. She too first believes changing his behavior would be easiest, but then her emotional intelligence kicks in. She realizes, "Do I really want to be with a guy who doesn't want to be with me, at least not as much as I want to be with him? Do I not deserve better? I'm better off single!" Then, in her case too, the negative voice will kick in. She may think, "Yeah, but that means I'll be single forever. I might never ever find a great guy..."

She knows this is just a mind game her negative voice will play. That's what negative voices do, just like the little devil that always floats around the heads of cartoon characters.

So she makes up her mind and thinks, "I don't care. If I'll be alone forever then so be it. I'm a great girl, and I'll find a great man. The only way to never find him is to stay with a guy who doesn't deserve my attention." And off she goes.

Great men have a radar for this. They love women with self-respect since they have a lot of it themselves. Having a lot of self-respect is an important high-value signal. It cannot be faked, botoxed, or implanted. You've either taken the time to develop it, or not. Self-respect is like a muscle. It needs to be trained if you want it to be strong since it's easier to take the path of no self-respect and to adapt.

Keep a great guy by paying attention to what matters most to him

Do you know what men want most from their girlfriend or wife? What, above everything else, is most important to them? Please think about the answer for a second, before you continue reading.

They want to feel like a man, not like a pussy or a wussy. All men have ever done since the age of ten is try to matter. This means trying to make sure to not be picked last in gym class when teams had to be formed. Trying to get girls. Trying to achieve. Trying to become someone. Men always try to matter. All great men have this built into their genes.

As they get older, this masculinity starts to evolve in a strong will to provide and protect. Simply put, most men want to build a nest, find a great wife who wouldn't mind living in that nest, make babies with her, care for her, provide, and protect. I start to see more and more men who don't want the baby part, but what *all* great men have in common is that they want to care for you. This is interesting because this means if you meet a guy who's seemingly not into caring for you, he's either not a great guy or not sufficiently interested in you.

A great way to keep a guy is to not only keep his masculinity intact but to also help him build it even stronger. This is something the high-value woman understands very well. She will give him what he needs. Not because she wants to manipulate him, but because she loves him so much she wants him to be all that he can be. He will do the same for her.

Men are attracted to your femininity. That's exactly what triggers their will to protect and provide for you. Sure, we live in a day and age where you no longer *need* it, but let him protect and care. He needs it more than you do.

What this means to him will be different for every guy you'll meet. There's no standard. What you'll most often see is that if you talk about any problem you face, he'll try to fix it for you. That's his way of caring and protecting. Some women don't like it when their guy tries to help. That's a mistake. It's best to let him take care of at least some of your challenges and problems.

Nonetheless, he's also going to do things that seemingly have nothing to do with you. He wants to show off and make you proud of him (by getting a raise, launching a new business, or achieving any other goal). This is a critical one. I've coached far too many women who failed to recognize how important these were to their guy. Remember how I explained that most men remain the three-year-old kid version of themselves to some degree? That part wants to get praise from the most important female in his life. This used to be mommy, now it's you. He will come home from work and explain how he successfully completed a certain task, gave a presentation, or achieved just about anything. Please listen to him and praise him for it. Even though you don't get what all the fuss is about. Just like a cat can bring home something it caught to make you proud, men will do the same. They might bring something home you don't need or care about at all. Still, they did it for you.

And that's exactly why it's so critical. You might think, "Well yes, that doesn't matter to me. I don't want him to work harder and earn more money. I'd rather have him spend more time with me." Although it doesn't look like it on the surface, he's still doing it for you. He will provide and protect in any way he sees fit. Please let him. He needs it to feel masculine.

This is a two-way street. He only deserves your praise and attention as long as he's giving you what you need. He will most often give back by committing more and more to you and openly showing his affection and love. I want to be clear, you should not support a guy who fails to show up for dates because of work, or a guy who disrespects you in any way. I'm talking about the good guy, who loves you, is affectionate, *and* works hard on his career in order to provide for you.

This is a positive vicious cycle. The more he can feel masculine around your feminine energy, the more he'll start to get addicted to you and the more he'll want to stay forever. He wants to matter to the woman he loves.

I've got a pretty poignant example of this. Dr. Mark K. Goldstein, a psychologist, did clinical research on the conditioning of husbands by their wives. He especially focused on angry and neglected wives. Here's what he wanted to find out: "Is there anything we've learned throughout years of research on how to influence *all* types of living organisms from as little as bacteria to as large as humans that we can test and apply on bad and sometimes even brutal husbands? Could we influence their behavior?"

Before the test on these husbands took place, research had shown that the best way to influence the behavior of anything that's alive is to reward the desired behavior instead of punishing the bad and undesired behavior. I've already discussed that earlier in this book. Punishment seems to work in the short term, but never does in the long term because resentment or at the very least indifference starts to appear. They had already tested this on pigeons and other animals, now it was time to test it on...men.

For this experiment, Dr. Goldstein sought out wives who had ordinary marital conflicts—nothing special. What all of these wives had in common, however, was that they kept focusing their attention on the undesirable behavior by either trying to punish it (nagging, complaining, fighting) or worse by rewarding the bad behavior by trying even harder to please their husbands. Both methods always backfired in the long run.

One wife in particular, let's call her Sabrina, presented an interesting case. After years of being in an unhappy marriage, Sabrina's husband finally left her...to move in with his new girlfriend. Interestingly enough, he kept calling Sabrina every now and then to see how she was. So he clearly still had somewhat of an interest in her. This is obviously crucial.

Now the question was, could Sabrina, for the sake of this experiment, influence the behavior of her ex-husband after he had already left her? Her strategy was to be different compared to what she had tried during the marriage. She would reward good behavior and stay indifferent to bad behavior.

Her first goal was to see if she could increase the frequency of his calls to her. Sabrina never called him; she was always on the receiving end. When he did call, she was very affectionate and positive. She complimented the things she *did* like about him (by encouraging him, complimenting him, praising him) and neglected what she didn't like (e.g., the fact that he left her after many years of marriage to move in with a new girlfriend). Sabrina meticulously recorded everything that happened—when he called, for how long, what they talked about, and more.

She was never critical, hostile, or negative, and she also always made sure that *she* was the one ending the calls. It didn't take long before the frequency of the phone calls increased significantly.

One day, he arrived at her house and stood at her door. Following the plan of the experiment, Sabrina said, "I'm so glad you're here. I have a fresh, imported Cuban cigar for you in the freezer, just the kind you like."

Sabrina continued to reinforce his good behavior (everything she liked) and paid no attention to the negative behavior. That very negative behavior, like his indifference, melted away automatically, and it didn't take long before he left his new girlfriend and asked if he could move back in. This is a prime example of how much power you have over men as a woman, if you play your cards right.

Reinforce the positive behavior. Don't give any (negative) attention to the bad behavior. If he shows bad behavior, lower your attention and withdraw. If he shows too much bad behavior to your liking, kick him to the curb.

Furthermore, this experiment proves how important it is to any man to be encouraged and praised by his girlfriend or wife. That's what attracts him the most!

Before I end this chapter, here's an important remark. Your female tenderness, praise, and devotion should be earned. If you start to compliment and praise him too soon, it will reek of desperation.

What I discussed in this chapter should only kick in when you are in an exclusive, committed relationship with your great guy who has been affectionate. It also helps to recuperate a relationship that started to go bad, but I wouldn't use it on a man who has shown a lack of interest from the get-go.

High value, not high maintenance

Some of what I've been explaining might make you believe the high-value woman is high maintenance since she seems to have a lot of rules men have to live up to. She is, in fact, not high maintenance at all. She has a ton of self-respect and self-love, and she will protect it dearly. But that's about it.

First of all, she almost never nags or complains. If she doesn't like something her guy does, she will accord less time and attention to him, but she sure understands that relationships require work, hard work. This means she needs to adapt just as much as he will have to. She doesn't make it any harder on him than she has to. She knows that wanting it your way all the time is for eight-year-old girls.

This is hard, isn't it? There's an eight-year-old girl in all of us. In me, too! I'd love it if the entire world would continuously adapt to me and my every whim. Some people, however, truly expect this and get frustrated when it doesn't happen. I'm sure you're not one of them, but I'm sure you know a couple of people who expect this. They are the ones continuously frustrated.

Flexibility is important, for your own sake. Not being flexible is the easiest way to be unsatisfied and frustrated.

Making sacrifices in relationships

This is a tough subject because we obviously all need to make sacrifices in a relationship. Where do you draw the line then? Before I dig into what the high-value woman would do, let's first look at what *not* to do.

Many people are brought up as a so-called Nice Guy or Nice Girl. They believe if they are good to the world and anyone in it, the world will be good to them too. Needless to say, that's not how the world works. So these well-meaning people are often left frustrated and feeling helpless.

Question is, are they *that* well-meaning?

It turns out they are not. Dr. Robert Glover, a psychologist, has studied the behaviors of Nice Guys for a very long time, and he concludes that Nice Guys are actually not that *nice.* They manipulate the women they are with. They try to *get* something from them (affection, sex, love) by being nice to them. They're not just nice to be nice; they want something in return.

Have you ever been with someone like that? Most women I've met, coached, or interviewed wholeheartedly confirm that being in a relationship with this type of guy feels very suffocating, as if he always wants something from you that you cannot give. Some of these women even asked their then boyfriend to "grow a pair" or to get a backbone.

This backbone is important. The nice people I talk about in this chapter allow people to walk all over them, often not only in their romantic relationships. They have a hard time saying no; they quickly get a feeling of guilt when they have to disappoint someone, and because of this, they are easily played by others.

Did you ever try to get more attention from someone (especially from a man) by being extra nice to him? If so, this chapter applies to you.

Nice guys and nice girls continuously emit signals that they are low value. They keep adapting their behavior, seek the approval of others, and let other people walk over them. No one, women or men, likes that in a romantic relationship unless they are the type who loves whips, chains, and dungeons.

You can be nice nevertheless. High-value men and women are nice, but they will always enforce their boundaries and when someone tries to walk over them. They'll be assertive (still in a kind way) and say no.

Tabitha, one of the women I coached, had a hard time applying this. She had an aversion for fights and discussions. Growing up, her dad had always been very strict and demanding. She tried to be a good girl to get his attention and kept that behavior as she became older and started dating men. These men, even the good guys, walked all over her because she let them. When Harvey, the boyfriend she was with when I coached her, did something she disliked, she never mentioned it. She got mad inside, but in order to not lose his praise and to steer clear of any fights, she neglected to be assertive. Every now and then, it would get too much for her and then she would explode and start yelling. Harvey didn't get where all of *that* was coming from, of course. Tabitha had to learn how to be assertive and immediately state what was important to her, instead of letting it build up.

That's what she started to do. She had reached out to me the moment where it was almost too late. Harvey had already told her he thought it would be a good idea for them to start seeing other people. I asked her to be much more assertive and state clearly what she wanted, without pointing the blame. That's what assertion is all about.

"I don't like it when you, because..."
Instead of "Why do you never..." or "Why did you..." That's pointing the finger and a sign of aggression. Assertiveness is all about "I," not showing what the other person did wrong.

As Tabitha started to apply this, the attraction (both the physical and emotional type) of Harvey started to rise again. Men love high-value women who assertively state their rules without getting mad, nagging, or any of the bad ways of communicating your needs.

You'll always need to make sacrifices in any relationship; he will have to as well. But you can never forgo what is truly dear to you. If you have to then he's not the *right* guy for you.

This too is where high-value women make the difference. They think ahead. They know that if they would adapt or change in order to please their guy or make him stay, *they* themselves will eventually become deeply unhappy. That's never on their agenda.

Pick your battles. If a change is easy to make and you wouldn't mind making this change for the rest of your life, go ahead and make the sacrifice. If you feel a ton of resistance coming from the core of who you are, it's better to not make that big of a sacrifice because you'll start to resent him. Assertively state what's important to you. If *he*'s then unable to adapt, he might be a great guy, but he's not the *right* guy for you.

This is often a tough nut to crack, and that's exactly where high-value women keep making the difference. Stepping out of a relationship with no future is darn hard on them, too. Yet, they do it since they understand it's necessary for their own long-term wellbeing.

Is he *really* in it for the long term?

To put it bluntly, men look for sex; women look for commitment. That's what we've been programmed to do, straight out of the box. This, of course, doesn't mean men don't need commitment and women don't need sex. But if we'd look at the primary motivators, these would be it.

Commitment will never be as high on his list as it will be on yours. So there will be a point where you can't help but wonder, "Is he as invested in our relationship as I am? Does he really love me? Is he really in it for the long term?" Your mind will start to look for signs and clues to get an answer. That's dangerous since these thoughts originate from a fear that, once passed onto the guy, will make him run. That's what I've described in detail in my book *Are You Scaring Him Away?* The sooner he'll sense this anxiety, the harder he will run. The more you force him to keep confirming he's in it for the long run, the more you are actually forcing him to question it.

High-value women have the same doubts in the back of their minds, but this is when their emotional intelligence kicks in. They don't act upon every negative emotion like fear or insecurity; they feel and they think about the long-term consequences of their actions.

Continuously seeking proof of his love and trying to take away the insecurity that every relationship comes with will eventually push every guy away (and great guys sooner than later).

High-value women know this Holy Grail doesn't exist. The security most women look for does not exist. Any man can at any time decide he wants to bolt from the relationship.

So can you. And this is exactly one of the many reasons why she's so attractive to high-quality men. They love her emotional strength.

Let me be vulnerable here. I'm a guy who suffers from a fear to commit. I've had a horrible childhood where my mother was yelling at my dad every day, telling him things like "Sleeping next to you every night makes me sick." Yet, my dad kept enduring this, for over ten years, until my mom finally called it quits. I made a promise to myself to never ever fall into the trap my dad had fallen into. I had a difficult time trusting women; this was one of my limiting beliefs instilled upon me during my childhood.

Whenever a relationship became a bit too serious, I started to withdraw automatically. Most women I dated did the wrong thing; they started to push me even more. That's the last thing you need to do with a guy who has real commitment issues.

My current long-term girlfriend of four years dealt with it in a different way: the high-value way. Here's exactly what happened. We had been dating for two months, and the relationship started to get serious. One night, right before going to bed—she had been staying over at my place the last couple of days—she said something simple that triggered my commitment alarm. I forgot what it was. She could sense I was withdrawing and becoming distant. Instead of saying, "Is everything all right? Do you still love me? Are you still serious about us?" or any of those pushy sentences, she said, "Would you like me to leave and stay at my own place?"

Wow. This got me thinking and snapped me right out of my commitment fear. "No, no. I have some commitment issues, but no, I want you to stay" is how I responded. She used the same response as we were packing up her stuff to move in with me, as I've already explained earlier.

Her self-confidence made me more attracted to her than ever. It raised her value significantly. She was not desperate or needy; she wouldn't ever get clingy. That's what her response communicated to me. She had options. If our relationship wouldn't work out for any reason or another, she would bump right back up and go on with her life. This is what attracted me. Can you see why? It's the exact opposite of the neediness men fear so much. All men, not just those with real commitment issues like myself.

Quick note about a man's fear to commit. I have had real issues with commitment. But a ton of guys and players just bring it up so they can keep playing with other women too.

If a man brings up the fact that he's not ready for a relationship early on and his actions are not proving his willingness to keep moving forward with you, he's not lying. Believe him and move on. He won't change. You're not the right girl for him. If you continue with a guy like that, you'll have to continue fighting a fight you cannot win.

You, super woman, deserve the best!

How does this title resonate with you? Is this something you believe? Do you actually deserve the best? Or has it happened that you've settled for less?

I honestly think we all have.

This is very dangerous in relationships because, before you know it, you've wasted years of your life with the wrong guy.

This makes me think of Karen. She was 46 when she asked for my help. A mother of two, she had been divorced twice. And both times she had been cheated on by her husband. Karen was attractive, witty, smart, and had everything she could want...except a great love life. When I dug a bit deeper, it became apparent that every single relationship she had ever been in followed the same pattern. The guy was very interested at first, but soon after, he took her for granted...and she let him!

I've explained before that men will always try to find out how far they can go—even the good guys. As I kept asking why she accepted the disinterest her boyfriends and husbands clearly showed, why she stayed with those men she responded, "I think I don't deserve any better." That was her belief and her entire love life had been a reflection of it.

Men will always treat you the way you allow them to. They cannot respect a woman more than she respects herself. And that's the interesting part. The high-value woman believes she deserves the best. A bit like the tagline Mercedes started to use around 2014: "The best or nothing." That's her motto. She wants a good and fulfilling relationship and if that's not possible, she'd rather have fun alone.

What is your belief about what you deserve? Do you truly believe you deserve the unconditional love of a man who won't go from hot to cold all the time?

I'm using the word "deserve," not "want." Most women *want* unconditional love. Question is, do they believe they *deserve* it? If you just want it, it will be easy to complain, nag, get mad, or use any form of influence you can think of to change a man's behavior. It will also be easy to let any bad behavior pass. But if you deserve it, you'll walk away from the men who cannot give you what you deserve.

A high-value woman never has to wonder where she stands with a guy. It won't come that far. Any guy who doesn't show her unconditional interest and love will be filtered out long before. She has better things to do. That's what finding a great relationship is all about, by the way. Putting a lot of men through a funnel and filtering out the one guy who's what you're looking for.

"I'm not ready for a relationship"

I've already touched on this subject before, but let's get into the nitty gritty. How would the high-value woman respond to a guy saying, "I'm not ready for a relationship?" *if* it's actually a great guy saying this? A guy she'd love to continue on with?

1. She dumps *him.*
2. She gets mad.
3. She tries to *sell* him on the idea of giving it a try.
4. She starts to put in a bigger effort to increase his attraction.
5. None of the above

Please think about the answer for a second, before you continue.

Option 1 would be the correct answer if this guy would have given her any red flags, but that's not the case here. This *is* a great guy, who simply seems scared or not ready to commit for any or no reason at all.

The correct answer is obviously not getting mad or trying to put in a bigger effort to increase his attention since this would only lower her value. It's not trying to sell him on the idea of giving it a try. This too would lower her value and, on top of this, make him withdraw. Can you see why?

We all love to buy, but we hate to be sold. If something needs to be sold upon us, our defense system kicks in and we start to wonder what's wrong with it.

So the correct answer was 5, none of the above.

Here's what the high-value woman would say: "If that's how you feel then I believe we should indeed stop seeing each other. I deserve a guy who's all in. You should take your time to figure out what you want and go have some fun. The fun you seem to be wanting. The fun a real committed relationship might exclude. So go ahead. And if we're meant to be, we might still get back together if I'm not in a committed relationship with another guy by that time."

This is a sneaky and powerful strategy. He has his doubts. She's not selling him on anything. On the contrary, she's reacting in the last way he would have ever expected. She's giving him the freedom he believes he needs right away, but there's one caveat. She adds, "If I'm not in a committed relationship with another guy by that time." This immediately triggers the "Indeed, what if she *is*?" response in him.

This is a strong response. It shows a ton of self-love and self-respect. It communicates, "Hey, I'm not going to try to keep someone around who doesn't want to keep me. I'll find someone else." But it's also loving since it says, "I care about you being happy. I appreciate you enough to not be selfish and give you what you requested" (even though I then decide to not be a part of it). And on top of that, it's a strong sign of self-respect: "I deserve someone who's all in." If that's not you, then I'll find someone who is.

Is this easy?

No, not at all. Your intuition will try to push you to plead, sell, nag, or feel frustrated. The high-value woman feels this too, and it's exactly because she moves past that and shows a ton of emotional intelligence that she indeed shows what enormous amounts of value she has. She clearly *is* a high-value woman. And only dumb guys will fail to notice this. The guys you wouldn't want anyway. Great men cannot help but feel respect for this type of woman.

When it's over, be gone

We all get one chance per person, per lifetime. High-value women get that and move on. It's true. Look around you. If you see examples of people getting back together after a breakup, you'll see them breaking up again later down the road, for the *exact* same reasons that lead to the first breakup.

Yet, so many women stay emotionally attached to their ex, working on strategies to get him back. This is a waste of energy. High-value women will never try to keep someone who doesn't want *them* around. This is too a sign of self-respect and dignity.

It will hurt, deeply. You can cry about it, feel depressed for a couple of weeks, but these are the types of wounds that time *does* heal. But the wound can only heal if you stop picking at it. This means **no contact** whatsoever with the ex. No subtle messages with a question mark in it in hopes of getting a sign of life from him. Nothing.

All that will do is point out to him that he made the right decision leaving you since these are clear signs of having no self-respect. He wants a strong woman, and this here is weak behavior. Men don't walk away from a woman lightly. When they *do*, they have made up their mind. They want someone else, someone different, someone better than who you were during that relationship. The more you'd then start to push him, the more you will prove he made the right decision. He can get better.

That's a stupid tendency most men have, even the great guys. Give them a Porsche, and they'll think they can get their hands on an even more expensive supercar. To put it bluntly, again, if a man can get his hands on what men would call a 7/10 without too much effort, he'll believe he can get an 8, maybe even a 9 *with* effort. If he breaks up with you or rejects you and you keep handing yourself over on a silver platter, thus making it super easy to get you, you are forcing him to realize he *can* get better than you (even if he really can't and is the dumbest idiot alive). He has made up his mind.

Protect your dignity and self-respect as if your love life depends on it. It does. When it's over, be gone.

When his attention declines

This is an important chapter. There's usually a moment in any relationship when his attention will start to decline, when the new has gone and everything has settled in.

You come home from work, but he'd rather watch Netflix than talk about your day. You put on something sexy, but he'd rather check his emails than look at you. Would this worry you? Would this make you believe he's losing interest?

You bet.

Nevertheless, this may not be the case. Even a highly interested guy will eventually suffer from the declining-attention syndrome. It's human nature. When Santa comes by and gives the three-year old boy a nice toy, he'll play with it for a couple of days, weeks at the most, until he slowly starts to pay less attention to it. Is he no longer interested in his toy?

Well, try to take it away from him and see what happens. "John, I see you're no longer playing with your new toy. I'm going to give it to the neighbors' kids, OK?"
Little John won't hesitate and will react as quickly as a chameleon can catch a fly. "No no, mommy! I still love it!" And you know what? He does! Question is, would it help if his mommy said, "John? Why don't you ever play with your new toy? It's as if you don't like it anymore." Of course not. It's difficult to steer the behavior of a guy using words alone.

And there's more! Little Johnny knows mommy seems to love the new toy too, so she's most surely *not* going to take it away. He has allllll the time in the world to play with it whenever he wants in the future, so why the rush?

Grown men are no different.

As I said, there inevitably comes a point in the relationship where he starts to take certain things for granted including the woman he's with. Trying to talk about it is the worst thing you can do. Can you see why?

It's a value-problem, yet again. The woman who nags and complains has just devalued herself, putting *him* in the stronger position and giving *him* all the power. The woman who nags has just proven that she will not walk away; otherwise, she would have.

Think of the toy again. The reason little Johnny gets bored of it is a) because he has played with it for a while and got used to it and b) he knows he'll have the toy indefinitely, unconditionally. So why hurry?

What if Santa would have told little Johnny that he gets the toy, but that one day the toy will disappear and be gone forever? Do you think little Johnny would let the toy out of sight, even for a second? Of course not! He would sleep with it under his pillow, attached to his wrist with a little cord...just to make sure.

Men start to take a woman for granted and start to give her less attention the moment they are sure she will stick around. This has everything to do with his hierarchy of needs. Most men want to be with a great woman. So finding her is very high on the hierarchy of needs. They'll put in a lot of time, money, and effort. Once that mission has been completed, that great woman has been found, attracted, dated, and now "relationshipped," he can focus more on his other needs again...like Netflix indeed.

This does not necessarily mean she's less important to him! He simply considers it a mission completed.

Women who love to nag will then take out their nagging rulebook and say, "You used to think I was sexy in this" or "Why don't you open doors for me like you used to when we just started dating?" or "We used to go for long, romantic walks, but you never have time for those anymore."

That's where the high-value woman plays it differently. With her, the mission is never ever completed. She might vanish anytime, and she will most surely never ever nag. All of the phrases from the nagging rulebook prove one thing to the guy, "I've got her. She's not going anywhere." Both the bad *and* the good guys will think it and will devalue the woman they're with. And you know what? Women do the exact same thing with nagging guys.

Nagging is like bluffing. A woman who nags has just proven that she won't run. She'll wait. And that's the exact opposite of what he needs. He needs you to withdraw a bit, without an explanation!

Let me repeat: don't use words when you want to change a man's behavior! Withdraw a bit for small infractions and a lot for major infractions. No words needed. Talking about it doesn't help anyway. Men can't talk about these things since they mostly don't have a clue of what they're feeling anyway.

Remember, reinforce the good behavior, ignore him when he shows unwanted behavior. Ignoring is the worst punishment you can give a child and even an adult. There's a tribe in Africa where, instead of giving criminals the death penalty, they are to be ignored by everyone, as if they no longer exist. Nobody looks at them; nobody talks to them. It's as if they became invisible ghosts. That's worse than death.

Long story short, when his attention for you starts to wane, do the same. Withdraw. This will peak his interest because it's unexpected. He expects you to nag! He doesn't expect you to withdraw. If you withdraw, he'll wonder what's going on and, regardless how long you've been together, will start chasing you more.

Take his toy away.

If and when he asks why, *then* you can talk. That said, don't show him the playbook. Don't say, "Well, I decided to spend less time with you because you seem to have lost interest in me." Instead say, "We were spending so much time together that I needed some space to (spend more time with friends, spend time on me, etc.)."

Here's why this works: **men know how to treat women well!** They do it all the time when they're out on a first, second, and maybe still the third date. Soon after, Alzheimer starts to kick in and they seem to forget how to treat a woman right. Here's a secret: they haven't forgotten! He knows he's not treating you as well as he should. He expects you to nag about it, all of his exes did! If and when you don't nag, *his* alarm bells will go off. He'll start to worry and will have concerns. Your reaction will be so unpredictable that it will make him wonder what he should do to be better.

Men lose attention when they feel secure, when they are sure you won't leave. Take away this security whenever you want to increase his attraction. This is a powerful weapon! The high-value woman never misuses it. It's her automated reaction whenever he takes her for granted, disrespects her, or does any of the other no-nos.

Abraham Maslow, quite an interesting fellow you might have heard of, came up with the hierarchy of needs. We all have one. It's a pyramid of needs and when one need is met, we start to worry about the next need. A simple example of this hierarchy of needs would be this: say you have some problems in your business. You found an unmet need and worry about it; you ponder and look for a solution. You come home from work, you open the fridge, and it's totally empty. Nothing to eat and you happen to live in the only town where no takeout or restaurant food can be found. On top of that, all the shops are closed and will be for the next seven days because of a strike...in your entire state. Finding food to eat will become a major and semi-urgent need. You'll put the problems at work aside and start to use your mental resources on finding something to eat. Or just imagine what would happen if you were scuba diving and somehow your air supply is cut off. That would be a major need, wouldn't it?

We all have a pyramid-like hierarchy of needs. When the basic needs have been met (oxygen, water, food), we start to worry about finding a roof over our heads. When we get that, we worry about what furniture to buy. When *all* of the basic needs have been met, we worry about our jobs, or our love life.

Men have this hierarchy of needs as well. Somewhere in his pyramid you'll find, "find a good woman who adores me." When that need has been met, he goes on to a higher layer of the pyramid like "What seats should I get for the Sunday football game?" or "How can I get a promotion?" or "John and I should really go out for drinks to catch up." He can worry about these because a more basic need, find a good woman who adores me, has been met. As long as he feels sure and secure about this need, he moves on to more specialized needs.

I think you see the strategy I'm about to explain, but I want to make sure you get that you can only use it sparingly. If you need to use this strategy monthly or worse, weekly, you're not with the right guy.

So here you are, in a relationship with a guy who starts to find going out with friends, work, or anything else *more* important than you. It might be that you're dealing with a bad man, someone who's stringing you along. These types of men I've described in my other book *Red Flags, Signs He's Playing Games with You*, but in this book, I'll presuppose he loves you and cares about you. When he moves on to other things, it's simply Maslow's hierarchy of needs at play. So what you can do is make him downshift in his pyramid.

He will *only* be able to enjoy his friends, work, golf, football, whatever *if* he's sure and secure about your feelings for him. That's why and when you withdraw, he'll put his full attention on you again. He has a major unmet need and wants to fix it, he'll seek your reassurance.

Did I ever tell you the story of walking my dog in the woods? I love the psychology of all things alive, and I used to be fascinated by how we interact with dogs since we cannot really talk to them. "What was the fastest way to have a dog that behaves so well that movie-dogs could learn a lesson or two from him?" I always wondered.

One day I was out for a walk in the woods with my dog, and we're walking on a wide path with a line of trees on the left and the right. I unleashed my young dog and off he went, running straight ahead. Some new dog owners then panic and start to run after the dog. That's always a funny sight, isn't it? The dog thinks, "Hey great! My owner is running after me, so I can keep going, I'm leading the pack! Look at me, so young and already leading the pack!" These dogs feel too sure and secure.

So I applied a different strategy. I noticed my dog wasn't even looking back to check my location, so I hid behind a tree. I was purposely carrying a little mirror so I could still keep an eye out on him without being noticed. As he was far in front of me, he turned around, still sure up to that moment that I was simply following, as if I was part of *his* pack. I wasn't around, and he couldn't see me. He panicked and started to run back, trying to pick up my trace. He couldn't since I hadn't been there yet. He searched and searched until he finally found me, standing behind that tree. He was so happy and had been so scared that, from that day off, he always stuck around and if he was in front of me, he checked back every couple of seconds to make sure I was still there.

Well, you see where I'm going with this… *This* is exactly what the high-value woman does with the guy she's with. She makes sure he keeps checking she's still around. He keeps putting in an effort because he knows if he slacks, she might be gone.

A man should never ever be totally sure that you unconditionally love him. For if he is sure, he'll move on to the next item in his hierarchy of needs.

Emotional Intelligence, the secret key

I'm sure you've seen it. Emotional intelligence and thus self-control cut through anything. It's the great differentiator between the nice girls who always finish last and the high-value women in loving relationships, especially in the beginning.

Imagine this. You go out on a date with a guy you've just met. He opens the door for you. He's funny, interesting, doesn't boast, asks a ton of questions because he really wants to get to know you...If you could design the perfect first date, this would be it.

What will your thoughts be as you're brushing your teeth after a great kiss goodnight? Chances are, it will be something to the tune of "My God, this was perfect. After everything I've been through lately. Wow! He's unlike *any* other man I've ever met..." You wouldn't be the first woman to think like this...partially because of the oxytocin that might already be rushing through your body just because of that first kiss.

The high-value woman is human. She feels it, too! She also starts to wonder if he's the one. Then she differentiates herself from the nice girl by thinking, "Stop. These are just my emotions. Life is not a Disney flick. I don't know him well enough to feel all of these warm and fuzzy emotions. He might be the one. He might be a psychopath. I don't know yet. Anyone can keep up an act for the duration of a first date, even a bad actor does this effortlessly. I was showing my best side, too."

She doesn't stop there. This is not a game to her where she tries to lock her heart and act cold and uninterested. Her attitude is simple. She thinks, "I don't know yet. I'll let these emotions do what they do, but I won't act upon them. This can still go into every direction. I'm giving him the benefit of the doubt, and I'll enjoy it for as long as it lasts. And if it doesn't last, I'll find someone else."

The more you control your own emotions, the more you'll be able to control where *this* goes. The more you let your oxytocin and "he's the one!" feelings dominate, the more *he* will dominate. And what's great is that this laid-back attitude will attract him even more.

I hear you. Controlling your emotions is not easy. It just isn't. I've been practicing this emotional intelligence play ever since I read Daniel Goleman's book *Emotional Intelligence* many years ago. But here's the good news. This is like a muscle. If you've ever been to a gym, you might have noticed the weights you simply cannot pick up become easy to lift if you gradually work your way up to them, letting the muscle evolve and get stronger.

Our mind has neural pathways that we create by our habits. As you were a toddler, walking on your two feet required a great deal of mental energy. You had to consciously go over all of the steps to take your first steps. This gradually grew into a new neural pathway, a habit. Now your brain can do it effortlessly. Same goes with managing our emotions. It takes a lot of practice, but it becomes easier and easier until it becomes an effortless automatism.

So the next time a guy sweeps you off your feet or if you're currently under a guy's spell, make a conscious emotional intelligent decision. Say to yourself, "These are just feelings. It's like an energy going through my body, based upon my hormones and substances like oxytocin. These are **feelings**. They do not reflect reality. They might not even be real."

It's true by the way. Coming from a background of panic attacks and unnecessary anxiety, I know firsthand how easy it is to have feelings that are not real. When I was anxious, there was no tiger in front of me about to eat me alive, yet my body acted that way.

When your body decides to have crush on any man, there possibly is no "the one" in front of you, even though your body acts that way. Keep giving him the benefit of the doubt, but keep repeating that these are just feelings. You do not need to act upon them. Nice girls feel these feelings, immerse themselves in it, crown him "the one," and then give away their power to a guy who does not deserve it (yet). High-value women feel these feelings, decide they are just feelings, and use their rational mind, as they move forward to get to know him better.

Never ever ever take his bad behavior personally. This goes far beyond dating and relationships. Let me be Captain Obvious once again. When you're walking around in the city and someone yells, "You have ugly hair!" does this mean you *do* have ugly hair? Hell no!

How other people treat you tells a lot more about *them* and how they feel than it says about you. Unless you've been with a guy for a while and let him walk all over you, then it partially *is* your fault. Still, you shouldn't blame yourself. You can learn from it, move on, and decide to never ever make that same mistake again. That too is being emotional intelligent.

We all mess up and make mistakes. Question is, do we keep making the same mistake? The definition of insanity is doing the same thing and expecting a different result; that's not really emotionally intelligent behavior now, is it?

So the next time you feel any emotion when it comes to men, (good ones like love, semi-dangerous ones like infatuation, or bad ones like "I'm gonna crown him "the one"), take a step back and see it for what it is. Emotions. Nothing special. And most importantly, not always right!

Consciously and rationally decide what is best for your long-term life, and then try to stick to that path, regardless of what your emotions are telling you.

They live happily ever after or do they?

Don't you love it how every chick flick, romantic flick, well, just about any flick ends with the hero girl and the hero boy falling in love and sailing off into the known future of unconditional love and never ending happiness.

How many real people do you know like that? Chances are not a lot...maybe none. Probably none.

We all have our problems. Love is not unconditional, and the prince on the white horse does not exist. The high-value woman doesn't expect him to exist. She knows every man she meets will have flaws and imperfections, just like she does, and that's perfect. She wouldn't have it any other way.

This is where she finds her strength. She's never needy and manages her emotions pretty well because she sees right through them. She's living *her* life. She focuses on what's important to her. Even though she hopes to find a great man she can take along for the ride, it's not a must. It's not a need. She's happy either way. With or without her prince charming. This alone makes her very attractive to all the great men she meets.

Most importantly, she doesn't wait for a man to change. She doesn't accept any bad behavior. She doesn't take any excuses. She's just gone, living happily ever after.

Final words

Thank you for reading this book and for making it till the end. I hope you found it inspiring. I've loved writing it for you. I've spent years researching these topics and coaching women to get the results the high-value woman successfully achieves. I hope you'll use what I've described. You deserve the results that go with it!

If you didn't like anything in the book, please reach out to me on brian@21datingtips.com.

Did you like it? I sincerely hope so. Then please share your thoughts on Amazon so other women just like you can find out more about the book. Reviewing is easy. Go to the book by typing in the title in Amazon, scroll down to the review section, and click on "Write a customer review." You have my eternal gratitude.

Thanks for reading!

Brian

PS. **And if you want even more tips and strategies**, sign up for my FREE advanced tactics newsletter on ScaringHimAway.com and join the 63,531 women who already receive it.